Do we need the New Testament?

Letting the Old Testament Speak for Itself

JOHN GOLDINGAY

IVP Academic

An imprint of InterVarsity Press
Downers Grove, Illinois

InterVarsity Press
P.O. Box 1400, Downers Grove, IL 60515-1426
ivpress.com
email@ivpress.com

InterVarsity Press® is the book-publishing division of InterVarsity Christian Fellowship/USA®, a movement of students and faculty active on campus at hundreds of universities, colleges and schools of nursing in the United States of America, and a member movement of the International Fellowship of Evangelical Students. For information about local and regional activities, visit intervarsity.org.

Cover design: Cindy Kiple
Interior design: Beth McGill
Images: © Mazor/iStockphoto

ISBN 978-0-8308-2469-4 (print)
ISBN 978-0-8308-9847-3 (digital)

Printed in the United States of America ♾

Library of Congress Cataloging-in-Publication Data

A catalog record for this book is available from the Library of Congress.

P	23	22	21	20	19	18	17	16	15	14	13	12	11	10	9	8	7	6	5	4	3	2	1
Y	34	33	32	31	30	29	28	27	26	25	24	23	22	21	20	19	18	17	16	15			

CONTENTS

INTRODUCTION

Yes, of course, we do need the New Testament, but why? Why is the Old Testament not enough? By asking that question, I am reversing the one Christians ask under their breath, the question whether we need the Old Testament, or whether the New Testament isn't enough.

Two bishops once met in a bar (I expect it wasn't actually a bar, but it makes for a better story). The bishops were called Polycarp and Marcion. When Marcion asked Polycarp if he knew who he was, Polycarp replied, "I know you, the firstborn of Satan!"[1] We know about their meeting from the writings of another bishop, Irenaeus; all three lived in the second century A.D. and were originally from Turkey. Marcion had come to some beliefs that were rather different from those of "orthodox" bishops such as Irenaeus and Polycarp. Among other things, he believed that the teachings of Jesus clashed irreconcilably with the picture of God conveyed by the Jewish Scriptures—what we call "the Old Testament," but that title hadn't yet come into use (neither was there yet a "New Testament"). While Polycarp likely had in mind Marcion's more general beliefs, someone like me who is passionate about the Old Testament may be forgiven for a high five in response to this greeting. Indeed, I am tempted to sympathize with the views of Cerinthus, another Turkish theologian about whom Polycarp himself passes on a story.[2] Cerinthus was too enthusiastic about the Torah; among other deviant views, he taught that believers in Jesus were obliged to keep the law, otherwise they could not be saved. Polycarp describes how John, the disciple of the Lord,

---

[1] See Irenaeus, *Heresies* III.3.4.
[2] This story, too, appears in Irenaeus, *Heresies* III.3.4.

was one day going to bathe at Ephesus. He saw Cerinthus there and rushed out of the bathhouse without bathing, exclaiming, "Let us fly, lest even the bathhouse fall down, because Cerinthus, the enemy of the truth, is within."

Many Christians are sensitive to the issue Marcion raises. For discussion at the final class in each course I teach, I invite students to tell me the major questions they still have. At the close of the course on the Pentateuch, in particular, they regularly ask about fitting together differences between the Pentateuch and the New Testament. When they try to specify the differences, a handful of concrete examples recur:

- Turning the other cheek over against an eye for an eye
- Loving your enemies over against killing your enemies
- Being peacemakers over against being war makers
- Jesus acting in love over against God acting in wrath
- Worshiping without outward rites over against worship that emphasizes sacrifice
- A chosen people based on their choice over against a chosen people based on ethnicity
- A relationship with God based on grace over against one based on law
- Concern for the whole world over against concern for Israel alone
- Real access to God over against purely bodily access
- God's teaching written into our minds rather than written only on stone
- Jesus treating women as equals rather than as subordinate to men
- All things being clean over against rules concerning clean and unclean

In this book I will consider questions such as these, and also aim to reverse the direction of the questioning and consider some of the ways in which the Old Testament interrogates us.

It's common to speak in terms of there being a "problem" about the relationship of the Old Testament and the New Testament.[3] The difficulty in

---

[3]For instance, the first section of Graeme Goldsworthy's article, "Relationship of Old Testament and New Testament" (in *New Dictionary of Biblical Theology*, ed. T. Desmond Alexander and Brian S. Rosner [Downers Grove, IL: InterVarsity Press, 2000], pp. 81-89), is titled "The Nature of the Problem" (p. 81).

solving the problem lies in large part in the way it is formulated. You could say that the problem lies in people thinking there is a problem or in the way they formulate the problem, in assuming an exaggerated assessment of the difference between the faith and life envisaged by the two Testaments. Indeed, there are several different facets to the two Testaments' relationship. Further, one might observe that the differences within each Testament are as marked as the differences between them: for instance, the differences between the story in Genesis-Kings and the Prophets, or between the expectations of the Torah and of the Prophets, or between Ecclesiastes or the Song of Songs and pretty much everything else in the Old Testament, or the differences between the Gospels and the Epistles, or between Paul and James, or between Revelation and pretty much everything else in the New Testament. Conversely, the continuity between the Testaments lies (for instance) in the way the Old Testament story continues in the New Testament story, the teaching of the Prophets continues in the teaching of Jesus and of the Epistles, and the promises of the Prophets continue in the promises in Revelation.

My passionate enthusiasm for the Old Testament makes me want to turn the "problem" of the relationship of the Testaments on its head, and the first chapter of this book seeks to do so. The other chapters then give more detail on the considerations lying behind the assertions in the opening chapter.

In general, I am focusing on the two Testaments' own account of their story, without seeking to get behind that version to ask whether what actually happened was different or to seek to establish that at every point it does tell us what actually happened. My aim is to discover what the Scriptures themselves have to say. I'm working on a book on biblical theology, and you could also see this book as a statement of the assumptions that lie behind that book.

My enthusiasm for the pre-Christian Scriptures also makes me unenthusiastic about *the Old Testament* as a title for them, as it is inclined to suggest something out of date and inferior. Henceforth, I will usually refer to them as *the First Testament*. The question when the Torah, the Prophets and the Writings came to be called *the Old Testament* is tricky. In 2 Corinthians 3:14 Paul speaks about people reading the *palaia diathēkē*, which the King James Version translates "old testament" and the New King James Version "Old Testament." But the context suggests a reference to the old covenant (as the King James Version implies), not to the Scriptures that speak of this covenant. The regular New Testament term for the Torah, the Prophets and the Writings is simply *the Scriptures*. When Melito, yet another second-century figure in Turkey (he was bishop of Sardis), lists the "the books of the old covenant,"[4] then this complete phrase does refer to the First Testament, but the expression *old covenant* itself still refers to the old covenant. In the early third century, the African theologian Tertullian uses the expression *vetus testamentum*,[5] a Latin equivalent to *palaia diathēkē*, which it is also natural to understand as referring to the old covenant; Tertullian's regular term for the First Testament is simply *scripturae*. The first occurrences of *vetus testamentum* to denote the Scriptures of the old covenant seem to come in the commentary on Revelation by Victorinus, a bishop in what is now Slovenia, dating from about A.D. 260.[6] But then, Jerome comments that Victorinus wasn't very good at Latin.[7] In between Tertullian and Victorinus in the third century, however, Origen, the theological writer from Alexandria, frequently uses the two Greek expressions *palaia diathēkē* and *kainē diathēkē* to refer to the Old Testament and the New Testament, so until someone puts me right, I will regard him as the earliest known source of the expression. If I get put right, I will post something on my web page, www.fuller.edu/sot/faculty/goldingay, under "Interpretation."

Most of the chapters in this book go back to papers given to meetings of the Society of Biblical Literature and the Society for Old Testament Study, to the Conference of the Australian and New Zealand Association of Theological Schools, and to the Stone-Campbell Journal Conference, and I profited from the comments of participants in those occasions. I am also grateful to Kathleen Scott Goldingay and to my friends and colleagues Thomas Bennett, Daniel Kirk and Marianne Meye Thompson for reading all or much of the book in draft and for suggesting points that I might reconsider, which I have often done, though not necessarily in a way that will mean they agree with it. Thomas Bennett also produced the subject index. Translations from either Testament are my own, except where otherwise indicated.

---

[4]The quotation comes in Eusebius, *Ecclesiastical History* IV, 26.
[5]*Against Marcion* V, 5.
[6]Victorinus, *Commentary on the Apocalypse of the Blessed John*, on Rev 5:1.
[7]Jerome, *The Lives of Illustrious Men* 74; cf. the comments of F. F. Bruce, "The Earliest Latin Commentary on the Apocalypse," *Evangelical Quarterly* 10 (1938): 352-66.

Do We Need the New Testament?[1]

So why do we need the New Testament? In what sense is the First Testament incomplete? What's new about the New Testament? What difference would it make if we didn't have the New Testament?

Salvation

We need the New Testament because it tells us about Jesus. As regards what it vitally tells us about him, the New Testament itself suggests that the answer lies in what Jesus did and what happened to him. Half of the New Testament is occupied with telling his story (four times), with a special focus on his execution and his resurrection. Much of the other half of the New Testament focuses on explaining the significance of that story, with an even sharper focus on his execution and resurrection. His letting himself be killed and his resurrection were the ultimate expression of God's love and power. In these events God let humanity do its worst to him, and declined to be overcome by its actions; God was both willing and able to overcome it. The submission and the overcoming meant something for God. They constituted God's refusal to be overcome by humanity's rejection or rebellion. God was insistent on bringing to a consummation the purpose he had initiated from the beginning. To use Jesus' language, God was insistent on reigning in the world and on not letting humanity get away from him. So the submission and the overcoming were important for God. Because they embodied those facts about God, the execution and the resurrection also meant something for humanity. They indi-

---

[1] A revised version of a paper published in the *Stone-Campbell Journal* 16 (2013): 235-48.

cated to us the far-reaching nature of God's willingness to submit himself to us and the far-reaching nature of God's power.

What if God had not sent his Son into the world or not collaborated in his Son's submitting himself to execution or not brought about his resurrection? And what if we had not known about those events—what if the Gospels had not been written?

In a sense God did nothing new in Jesus. God was simply taking to its logical and ultimate extreme the activity in which he had been involved throughout the First Testament story. All the way through, God had been letting humanity do its worst. He had especially been letting the people he adopted do its worst, and had been refusing to be overcome by its rejection and rebellion, declining to abandon it or destroy it. God had been paying the price for his people's attitude to him, sacrificing himself for this people, bearing its sin. He had been absorbing the force of that sin, carrying it in himself rather than making Israel carry it. This carrying did not exclude disciplining Israel; but when God brought trouble on Israel, the trouble-bringing was an act of discipline within the context of an ongoing relationship like that between a parent and a child.

The fact that God had been acting in this way through Israel's story didn't make it redundant for God to bring his self-sacrifice to a climax in Jesus. This last self-sacrifice was the logical and inevitable culmination of that earlier way of acting and letting himself be acted on, the final expression of it. To be a little paradoxical, if God hadn't acted in this way in Jesus, he wouldn't have been acting in that way in Israel's story and in the world's story.

Through the story of the nations and through Israel's story God had been declaring that he was king, and he had sometimes been acting like a king in imposing his will on the nations or on Israel. That declaration and action was inclined to draw forth human resistance. The nations and Israel preferred to make their own decisions. The coming of Jesus constituted another assertion that God was king and that he intended to behave as king in relation to the nations and to the world, an assertion made in acts and in words. Predictably, Jesus' coming and his declaration about God reigning drew forth a response of resistance. The resistance was expressed in the execution of God's Son, which appropriately involved both the nations and the people of God. It constituted the ultimate expression of human wickedness. It thus drew forth the ultimate expression of God's submission to humanity. God remained sovereign Lord;

he was not compelled by any factors outside himself. Yet God deliberately let humanity do what it wanted to him, and did so under a compulsion that came from inside himself. It was a compulsion that derived from who he was, a compulsion to be himself. He could not deny himself or be untrue to himself (2 Tim 2:13). By the same dynamic, when we insisted on executing God's Son, this act also drew forth the ultimate expression of God's faithfulness and God's power, in resurrecting Jesus. One might almost say that God had to provoke humanity into its ultimate act of rebellion in order to have the opportunity to act in a way that refused to let this ultimate act of rebellion have the last word.

By the same dynamic again, our subsequent continuing resistance to God's reign as nations and as the people of God means Jesus must come back to implement that reign.

God's submitting his Son to execution was thus necessary for God's sake and for humanity's sake. It was necessary for God to be God in this way to fulfill his purpose and overcome human rebellion. In letting his Son die, God was being true to himself in undertaking this ultimate act of submission to human self-assertiveness, and refusing to be frustrated by it or to abandon humanity to its sinfulness or to surrender his relationship with humanity. It was necessary for humanity's sake in order to bring home to humanity the truth about itself and about God, and to draw it from rebellion to submission, from resistance to faith. As the point is classically put, the act of atonement had an objective and a subjective aspect.

Insofar as God's act was undertaken for God's sake, there was no great need for humanity to know about it. It could have been done in secret or not recorded. But insofar as it was undertaken for humanity's sake, as a demonstration of divine love, it needed to be done in public and it needed to be recorded, so that people two thousand years later can still be drawn by it.

So do we need the New Testament? It has been argued that "to say that the Hebrew Bible has complete integrity over against the New Testament is to cast grave doubts upon the unity of the Christian Bible. It is like saying that one can read the first ten books of the *Aeneid* as if the last two did not exist, and this, in turn, is to say that the last two add nothing essential."[2] My argument

---

[2]Jon D. Levenson, *The Hebrew Bible, the Old Testament, and Historical Criticism* (Louisville: Westminster John Knox, 1993), p. 101; cf. Harold Bloom, *Jesus and Yahweh* (New York: Riverhead, 2005), p. 115.

is that the execution and the resurrection were indeed the logical end term of a stance that God had been taking through First Testament times, so that the First Testament story does give an entirely adequate account of who God is and of the basis for relating to God. Because of who God has always been, God was already able to be in relationship with his people, despite their rebellion. God has always been able and willing to carry their waywardness. And on the basis of that story, Israel has always been able to respond to God and to be in relationship with God. In this sense the gospel did not open up any new possibilities to people; those possibilities were always there. Yet the dying and the resurrection were the ultimate expression of who the God of Israel is, and the story of the dying and the resurrection is the story of that ultimate expression of who the God of Israel is. They do therefore provide the ultimate public basis for responding to God and trusting in God. Abraham and Sarah, Miriam and Moses, Jeremiah and Huldah, Esther and Daniel managed okay without the New Testament, but we are privileged to have the story it tells because it gives us the climactic expression of the truth about God that they lived by.

Narrative

So is the First Testament story complete on its own? The New Testament story does add to the First Testament story, but so do other Jewish writings from the Greek and Roman periods such as 1 Maccabees. The movie *The Bourne Legacy* added to the earlier Bourne movies, but this fact does not signify that the earlier movies needed a fourth in the sequence.

The beginning of Matthew's Gospel implies that the story told in the First Testament and the story told in this Gospel can be read as a unified story, but it does so in a way that also indicates that the First Testament story does not have to be read that way. Matthew speaks of fourteen generations from Abraham to David, fourteen from David to the exile and fourteen from the exile to Jesus, which suggests that the story forms one elegant whole. But the First Testament itself shows that Matthew has been selective with its story in order to make the point. In the First Testament there were more than fourteen generations from Abraham to David and from David to the exile. Matthew is working backwards. He knows that Jesus is the climax of the biblical story, and he shapes it accordingly. But the shaping does not emerge from the First Testament narrative itself.

Paul likewise knows that he and his churches are living in the context of the climax in the biblical story, and it has been argued that this perspective "allows him to read the story whole from the standpoint of its ending, thus perceiving correspondences and narrative unities that would have been hidden from characters in the earlier chapters of the story." The "astonishing event" of the execution and resurrection of Jesus was then "completely unpredictable on the basis of the story's plot development," but it "is nonetheless now seen as the supremely fitting narrative culmination, providing unforeseen closure to dangling narrative themes and demanding a reconfiguration of . . . the reader's grasp of 'what the story is all about.'"[3]

Jesus' execution and resurrection may have been largely unpredicted on the basis of the First Testament story, yet Jesus didn't see them as unpredictable. He was not surprised at his execution and resurrection, and his lack of surprise did not simply issue from his possessing divine insight. His execution fitted the pattern of the First Testament story; Israel had regularly rejected and killed its prophets (e.g., Mt 16; 23). His resurrection, too, fitted the pattern of the First Testament story. Ezekiel 37 notes how Israel in exile saw itself as dead and hopeless, yet God brought it back from the dead and reestablished it in fulfillment of Ezekiel's promise that Israel would be raised from the dead. So the "astonishing event" of Jesus' execution and resurrection is a logical continuation and culmination of Israel's story, though we might not have seen that Israel's story is a story of death and resurrection unless we were reading it in light of Jesus' story.

There is then a converse point to be made. The First Testament indicates that God brings Israel back to life after the exile, but it also indicates that this new life is not as glorious as the life promised by Ezekiel's vision. The story in Ezra and Nehemiah portrays the community's reestablishment, but the story then peters out rather than achieving closure. In a sense the late Second Temple community is still living in exile,[4] yet the Jewish people is living throughout the historic borders of Israel, so I would rather speak of it seeing itself as still in need of restoration. The Holy Spirit thus inspires John the Baptizer's father to

---

[3] Richard B. Hays, *Echoes of Scripture in the Letters of Paul* (New Haven: Yale University Press, 1989), p. 100. In a footnote Hays acknowledges the influence of insights from Northrop Frye and Paul Ricoeur on this sentence.

[4] So N. T. Wright, e.g., *The New Testament and the People of God* (London: SPCK, 1992), pp. 268-72.

*The story of the OT: (+ Jesus)
rejection turned into redemption*

speak not in terms of exile and return but in terms of freedom, of light shining on people living in the shadow of death (see Lk 1:67-79).

Luke's version of the gospel story thus starts by suggesting that Jesus' coming will bring the downfall of Rome and the restoration of Israel to freedom and full life. "He has brought down rulers from their thrones," Mary says; he has "rescued us from the hand of our enemies," Zechariah says (Lk 1:52, 74). In the short term, this prospect gets frustrated by the leadership of the people of God, whose hostility leads to Jesus' execution. The process whereby God restores his people and implements his sovereignty in the world involves God letting that rejection happen and turning it into a means of achieving his purpose. The process God goes through in Jesus parallels the one God goes through in the First Testament story.

So Jesus comes to bring Israel back to fullness of life, and his own dying and rising is designed to bring its story to its magnificent conclusion. Yet it does not do so. Israel strangely declines that closure. Paul then sees a further mysterious divine providence in this refusal: it adds impetus to the carrying of the gospel message to the Gentile world, pending a closure for Israel that will come later. Yet, we can hardly say that the spreading of the gospel issues in a church that simply manifests resurrection life. The church engages in crucifixion (Christian groups kill one another); the church experiences crucifixion (Christians get martyred); the church experiences resurrection (churches sometimes die but come back to life).

The First Testament, then, reaches a partial closure, but not a complete one; the New Testament likewise achieves a partial closure, but not a complete one. This parallel gives the First Testament story more potential to be instructive for the church than is realized in the way people commonly think of this story. When Paul wants to get the Corinthians to reflect on their life, he points them to Israel's story as it unfolded from Egypt to the Promised Land, and comments that "these things happened to them as examples, but they were written for our admonition, on whom the end of the ages has come" (1 Cor 10:11). There might seem to be some tension in Paul's comment. If the end of the ages has come, would one expect there to be illumination for the church in these stories about Israel's experience before it reached the Promised Land? Yet the issues that arise in the Corinthian church's life show that living in the last days does not transform the life of the church. Israel's

As Ex + Prom land are to be pp.
so B our position btw Jesus + Parousia.

Do We Need the New Testament? 17

position between the exodus and the Promised Land provides a parallel for the church's position between Jesus' resurrection and his final appearing.

The First Testament story is not merely the history of our distant spiritual ancestors, a history of a period so different from ours that it hardly relates to our life now that the end of the ages has come. It is the history of a people like us in a position not so different from ours. Our pretense that things are otherwise puts us into potentially fatal jeopardy.

MISSION

Do we need the New Testament because the First Testament focuses exclusively on Israel and we would not otherwise know of God's concern for the whole world? In fact, God's concern for the nations goes back to the beginning. The First Testament relates how God created the whole world and was involved with the development of all the nations. The aim of God's appearing to Abraham was not simply to bless him but to drive the nations to pray for blessing like Abraham's. God's judgment of the Egyptians and the Canaanites does not mean God is unconcerned about other nations, as God's judgment of Israel and God's judgment of the church does not mean God is unconcerned about Israel and about the church. Prophets look forward to a time when nations will flock to Jerusalem to get Yahweh to make decisions for them. Psalms repeatedly summon all the nations to acknowledge Yahweh with their praise.

In keeping with this concern, the spread of the Jewish people around the Middle East and the Mediterranean before Jesus' day had the happy result that there were synagogues throughout those worlds, and these synagogues were attracting Gentiles to acknowledge Yahweh. In keeping with this concern, too, before Jesus' day the Jewish Scriptures had been translated into Greek, which issued in the translation called the Septuagint. Gentiles as well as Jews who did not know Hebrew could thus read them. The book of Acts relates a series of events that gave new impetus to spreading knowledge of the God of Israel: Pentecost, the abolition of the Jewish people's distinctive rule of faith as related in the Cornelius story and the broader process the book relates. Yet these events did not initiate the spreading of knowledge of Israel's God among the Gentiles. One might try a thought experiment. Suppose Jesus had not come when he did. What would have happened? Whether or not the Jewish community was deliberately seeking to spread knowledge of its God and its Scriptures, maybe Judaism would have continued to spread through the Gentile world and become more and more of a world religion.

God's strategy in seeking to fulfill his purpose for creation worked somewhat as follows. First he commissioned humanity to subdue and care for the world. It didn't work. So he tried destroying most of the world and starting again with one family. It didn't work. So he tried a third time with one family but separated them from the rest of the world in order to bless them so spectacularly that the entire world would pray to be blessed as they were blessed. This strategy also didn't work, and the descendants of Abraham and Sarah ended up back in the Babylonia from which they had come. God tried a fourth time by reestablishing the community centered on Jerusalem, though many people who had been scattered around the Mediterranean and Middle Eastern worlds stayed in the place of their dispersion or spread further. While this arrangement proved more effective insofar as these Jewish communities were in a position to attract many Gentiles to come to believe in the God of the Torah, the Jewish people centered on Jerusalem remained under the domination of the superpower of the day. So God tried a fifth time by sending his Son into the world. When this strategy again initially failed in particularly catastrophic fashion, God again transformed disaster into potential triumph. He turned the failure and his refusal to be beaten by it into a message that could go out to the entire world, making use of that already-existent dispersion of the Jewish community and the way it had already brought some Gentiles to believe in the God of the Torah.

The strategy of attraction that God had initiated with Abraham and Sarah continued. The focus of the Epistles lies on seeing that Christian congregations grow in their understanding of the gospel and their embodying of that gospel in their life. The world's coming to recognize the God of the gospel would then follow. Paul makes this vision of attraction specific to the Corinthians when he speaks of people coming to the congregation's worship, falling down to worship God themselves and acknowledging that "God is really among you" (1 Cor 14:26). The dynamic is the one envisaged by Zechariah, who pictures ten people from every tongue among the nations taking hold of the hem of every Jew's coat and saying, "We want to go with you, because we've heard that God is with you" (Zech 8:23).

When prophets promise that the nations will flock to Jerusalem, they don't imply that they will cease to be distinguishable nations and ethnic groups.

God had encouraged them to develop in their diversity, and it would be weird for them to cease to manifest the manifold wisdom of God in their differentiation. Likewise, when Paul declares that all are one in Christ Jesus (Gal 3:28), there is no implication that they are all the same; at least, it is not so with male and female. Paul is talking about the fact that everyone has the same way of becoming God's child. One would expect nations to remain distinguishable but to be able to rejoice in their diversity, and one would expect Israel's ethnic distinctiveness to continue, but this distinctiveness had never implied that Israel alone could know God, and neither would it do so after Jesus.

On the other hand, the people of God will no longer be a political entity over against other political entities. It had not been so in the beginning, in the time of the ancestors, though it had been so for the time from Saul to Jehoiakin, from the appointment of the first king to the deposing of the last king within the First Testament story. During the Second Temple period, Judah once again became a sort-of political entity, and Judah in a sense remained the heart or focus of the Jewish people, but from Jehoiakin's time onward, the Jewish people always constituted an entity that comprised both people in Judah and people dispersed among other nations. In the twentieth century Jerusalem again became the capital of a political entity, but there continued to be more Jews spread around the world than Jews living in the state of Israel. Israel was a political entity only for a few centuries. It is not essentially so. Jesus made no difference to that fact.

It is not the case that we need the New Testament because otherwise we would not realize that God cared about the whole world, nor because God's revelation to the Jewish people had not reached outside the Jewish community. The First Testament made clear God's concern for the whole world, and before Jesus' time, the Jewish people had been attracting people to the revelation in the Scriptures. In connection with the discipling of the nations (Mt 28:18-20), a major significance of the New Testament is that it opens windows into the life of a series of congregations spread around the Mediterranean and helps us to see the nature of the congregational life that embodies the gospel. But we have noted how Paul speaks to the Corinthians about the importance of learning from Israel's story, and another facet of that importance appears here. God's strategy was that his people would be the magnet that attracts people to him. Israel was not very good at being such a magnet, and the church continues to have this problem.

THEOLOGY

Do we need the New Testament because we wouldn't otherwise have as true
a revelation of God?

The classic way to make the point is to say that the First Testament gives
people the impression that Yahweh is a God of wrath and that we need Jesus
to show us that God is a God of love. This common understanding is hard
to reconcile with either Testament. Jews do not get the impression from their
Scriptures that Yahweh is a God of wrath. Yahweh is indeed capable of acting
in wrath, but the relationship of love and wrath in Yahweh is well summed
up in a line from the middle of Lamentations. According to the common
rendering, Yahweh "does not willingly afflict or hurt people" (Lam 3:33).
More literally and even more strikingly, Yahweh "does not afflict or hurt
people from his heart." Yahweh's heart is compassion and mercy, so that
when he afflicts or hurts, it doesn't come from the center of his being, but
from somewhere nearer the edge of it. It does not express who he is at heart.

Thus the New Testament doesn't say, "You know how the First Testament
gives people the impression that God is a God of wrath? Well, we can now tell
you that God is a God of love." It doesn't speak in terms of having new things
to say about God's character that the First Testament doesn't say. It doesn't
suggest that the "Divine fatherhood" is a "new truth . . . revealed to man in Jesus
Christ,"[5] or even that it brings "a radical deepening of the Old Testament doctrine of God" in which "'Father' is now revealed to be more than an epithet."[6]
It doesn't portray people such as the Pharisees or Jesus' disciples as having a
false or incomplete understanding of God before Jesus arrives, nor picture
them as responding with horror or surprise at things Jesus says about God,
except for tough things such as the idea that God might cooperate with the idea
of him being crucified or that God might expect them to stay married to the
same person for life (e.g., Mt 16:21-22; 19:10). It doesn't usually get the reaction,
"Oh, we could never have known God was like that, but now it's revealed to us."

There are New Testament texts that have been read that way, but they don't
bear further examination in this connection. John says that the law was given

---

[5]So J. Armitage Robinson, *St. Paul's Epistle to the Ephesians*, 2nd ed. (London: James Clarke
[1904?]), p. 83.
[6]So Thomas F. Torrance, "The Christian Apprehension of God the Father," in *Speaking the Christian God*, ed. Alvin F. Kimel (Grand Rapids: Eerdmans, 1992), pp. 120-43 (p. 131).

through Moses; grace and truth came through Jesus Christ (Jn 1:17). He hardly means that Moses didn't know about God being grace and truth. That very phrase sums up God's self-revelation to Moses in Exodus 34:6, which is then alluded to many times in the First Testament. The King James Version (among others) has the very words *gracious* and *truth* as part of its translation of the verse in Exodus. Grace and truth came through Moses in the sense that he treated these realities as the foundation of God's relationship with Israel— or rather, he reaffirmed that point, which Abraham also knew already. The relationship between God and Israel was based on God's grace. It required the response of obedience to God's expectations; but then, the New Testament also assumes that the relationship God initiates with us requires a response of obedience. Otherwise, there will be no relationship.

But neither Moses himself nor the Torah for which he stands was an embodiment of grace and truth in the sense that Jesus was, as the incarnation of God, as grace and truth on two legs walking around Galilee and Jerusalem. I recently took part in a long phone conversation with someone, and subsequently met the person for dinner. In a sense I learned nothing new on the dinner occasion, but meeting the person sure made him more real and fleshed him out. As John goes on, "No one has ever seen God, but a one and only son, God, who is close to the father's heart, he has given an account of him" (Jn 1:18). Being one who embodies grace and truth and being God's only son and being one who can give an account of God, Jesus *is* himself divine. He does not offer a new revelation of God in the sense of a different revelation, but he does give people a fresh one, providing them with an unprecedentedly vivid embodiment of the revelation they had. The gift that the New Testament gives is its story of God's known character embodied in someone visible, embodied in a concrete life.

The same insight emerges from the beginning of Hebrews. "God, having spoken in many different forms and in many different ways of old to our ancestors through the prophets, at the end of these days spoke to us through a son" (Heb 1:1-2). The point in Hebrews, too, is not that God has now said something different or something additional over against what he said through the prophets. It is that the different revelations given through the different prophets have now been embodied altogether in this one person.

This embodiment means that the New Testament does make the metaphysical questions about God more complicated. God is one; Jesus is divine; Jesus addresses the Father, so he is in some sense a different person from the Father; and the spirit of God or of Jesus brings the real presence of God or of Jesus to people. These facts in due course led to the formulation of the doctrine of the Trinity, to safeguard those truths about God, Jesus and the Spirit. Yet the doctrine of the Trinity didn't exactly add to people's knowledge of God. Suppose by another thought experiment we project ourselves back into the position of believers in First Testament times, or of believers living on the eve of Jesus' birth—people such as Elizabeth and Zechariah, Mary and Joseph, Anna and Simeon. What did they lack by not knowing about the Trinity? They knew that God was powerful and compassionate and just. They knew that he loved being in relationship with people. They knew he was a reality in their lives. They heard him speak. They knew they could pray to him. They knew the realities that the doctrine of the Trinity presupposes. I'm not clear they missed out too much by not knowing about the doctrine itself.

If one asks how the Trinity is positively significant for Christians, then a standard contemporary answer in the West is that it establishes the presence of relationality in God and of free collaboration within God.[7] Those deductions from the doctrine of the Trinity are contextual inferences that became important to Western thinkers in the late twentieth century because of our concern about relationality, a concern issuing from the fact that relationality is a problem to us culturally and philosophically.[8] Our contemporary Western context thus enables us to see that the doctrine of the Trinity brings out a scriptural truth about God. But God's relationality is not a truth that comes from the New Testament as opposed to the First Testament. It's there in both. The doctrine of the Trinity safeguards against error and enables us to see things in the Scriptures, but it doesn't exactly reveal new things.

RESURRECTION HOPE

I have been arguing that the New Testament tells us little that's new about God, though it tells us of a spectacular embodiment of the already-revealed

---

[7]See, e.g., Ted Peters, *God as Trinity: Relationality and Temporality in Divine Life* (Louisville: Westminster John Knox, 1993).

[8]For the latter, see Anthony C. Thiselton, *The Hermeneutics of Doctrine* (Grand Rapids: Eerdmans, 2007), pp. 231-40.

truth about God. There is a theological truth that is confined to the New Testament, a truth about hope. In the Torah, the Prophets and the Writings, the grave or Sheol or Hades is the termination of the story for human beings. It's not an especially nasty end (Sheol is not a place of punishment), but neither is it a very exciting one. In the New Testament, there is a bigger end to come after our death, an end that will mean our rising to a new life, with new bodies—or our going to hell. Those earlier Scriptures do not incorporate either aspect of this truth, the good news or the bad news.

They do include two slight hints of it, one at their beginning and one at their end. At the beginning, the first human beings have access to a life tree; if they eat it, they will live forever. Because of choosing to eat of another tree in disobedience to God's command, they and their descendants lose access to the life tree. So that story explains why we all die, and the wider story leaves there the fact that God originally intended us to live eternally. The other end of the First Testament, in Daniel 12, promises that many dead people will wake up again, some to lasting life, some to lasting contempt. It's the last scene in the First Testament, insofar as it has its background in the martyrdoms brought about by Antiochus Epiphanes in the second-century crisis in Jerusalem. Antiochus had banned proper worship of Yahweh and replaced it by pagan worship, and Jews paid with their lives for their faithfulness to God in that situation. It surely can't be the case that God simply lets such faithful servants be killed in this way and lets the unfaithful live on until they die in their beds. Daniel 12 promises that God will take action to reverse things. It's the only reference to a form of resurrection to life or death in the First Testament.

Notwithstanding the questions raised by its story about the life tree, the First Testament is content with the idea that this life is all we have. When people have lived a full life and are "full of years" (e.g., Job 42:17), they are content to go to be with their ancestors. They do not cease to exist but they go to Sheol, a place of a lifeless existence. The First Testament gives some accounts of dead people being resuscitated, but resurrection involves more than resuscitation. It involves a new kind of life that will not end in death, and it involves a spiritual body—that is, a body that lives according to the spirit and not according to the lower nature. Enoch and Elijah are taken to be with God, but their experience does not correspond to the resurrection of which the New Testament speaks. The Psalms chafe loudly about the way early death can be caused by undeserved troubles and the way people may not be able to live out their full life; but what they therefore seek is deliverance that makes it possible to live a long life, and the early death of people who threaten to cause undeserved death. The Psalms can speak about living in God's presence "forever," but the term *forever* can refer to the whole of a life (e.g., Ex 21:6; 1 Sam 1:22; 20:23; 27:12), and nothing elsewhere in the First Testament suggests that the Psalms would be referring to eternal life. "Forever" does not point to something beyond or better than Sheol.

Why did God not let the Israelites know about resurrection life? Perhaps he was concerned to get them to take this life really seriously. Once people know about eternal life, they often stop taking this life really seriously.[9] The history of Christian attitudes provides evidence for this speculation. We need the New Testament to give us hope for resurrection life, but we need the First Testament to remind us of the importance of this life, and to give us hope for this life.

It's appropriate that the First Testament should have no expectation of resurrection life, because until Jesus died and rose, there was going to be no resurrection. It's not that the First Testament was wrong; it was right. Jesus is the Second Adam. His death and resurrection initiates a new humanity. It was all very well for the hope of resurrection life to arise in the time of the Maccabees, but there was no basis for accepting it until Jesus died and rose from the dead. Hence the fact that Jesus went to make a proclamation to people who belonged to God but had died and were in Sheol (1 Pet 4:6); he went to give them the good news that they were not stuck in Sheol forever, after all.

When Jesus argued with the Sadducees about resurrection, he did urge that resurrection to life must follow from the reality of God's relationship with people. His argument also implies a possible reason for the reality of hell; perhaps hell must likewise follow from the lack of that reality. "Hell is other people," says one of the characters in Jean-Paul Sartre's play *No Exit*, a drama about three people who are in hell and thus can't escape one another. Hell is a matter of relationships—specific relationships, in the context of the saying in Sartre's play. To turn that idea inside out, Jesus' saying might imply that hell is the continuing lack of a relationship between God and people, the lack that characterizes their life now. The related implication of Daniel

---

[9]So Dietrich Bonhoeffer, *Letters and Papers from Prison* (reprinted London: Collins, 1962), pp. 50, 112.

12 is that it is appropriate for faithlessness to receive some more explicit exposure than the fact that people's life simply fizzles out. It is the reason why the realization about hell as well as that about resurrection developed in Judaism. Hell means judgment. Jesus is the person who introduces hell into the Bible, but he was taking up an idea present in Judaism by his day.

PROMISE AND FULFILLMENT

There is a broader question about hope in connection with the relationship between the Testaments. Does the First Testament relate the promises whose fulfillment is related in the New Testament?

It is an oversimplification to say that the First Testament witnesses to "a time of expectation" whereas the New Testament reflects "a time of recollection."[10] There is an interesting contrast in the order of books between the Torah, the Prophets and the Writings on one hand, and the "Old Testament" on the other. The order in the Christian Bible "posits a progressive movement through history toward an ideal of eschatological redemption in the messianic age," whereas the Torah, the Prophets and the Writings posit an ideal state at the outset with the building of the temple in the land, where the Torah can be implemented, a disruption with the exile, then a restoration with the temple's rebuilding.[11] The First Testament does indeed spend much of its time recollecting. But it also looks to the future for God's own action to implement his purpose. The New Testament, too, spends much of its time expecting. The Christian order of the books in the Old Testament, which broadly follows the Septuagint and puts the Prophets at the end, encourages the perception that it ends up looking forward in a way that the order Torah, Prophets, Writings does not. But it's not clear that in origin the order in the Old Testament is Christian rather than Jewish;[12] "it should not be forgotten that the Septuagint was a Jewish translation, not a Christian one."[13]

The First Testament certainly relates promises that are fulfilled within

---

[10]Karl Barth, *Church Dogmatics* I, 2 (Edinburgh: T & T Clark, 1956), p. 45; cf. Thiselton, *The Hermeneutics of Doctrine*, p. 63.

[11]Marvin A. Sweeney, "Tanak Versus Old Testament," in *Problems in Biblical Theology*, ed. Henry T. C. Sun et al., Rolf Knierim festschrift (Grand Rapids: Eerdmans, 1997), pp. 353-72 (p. 359).

[12]See, e.g., Klaus Koch, "Is Daniel Also Among the Prophets?" *Interpretation* 39 (1985): 117-30 (121).

[13]Brevard S. Childs, *Old Testament Theology in a Canonical Context* (Philadelphia: Fortress, 1986), p. 7.

its own time: for instance, Isaiah tells Hezekiah that the treasures of Jerusalem will be taken off to Babylon, along with some of Hezekiah's descendants (Is 39:5-7). It happens. Yahweh's proven capacity to declare what is going to happen, and then to make it happen, is a major reason for believing he is God (e.g., Is 41:1-7, 21-29). The New Testament, too, makes declarations about the future that are fulfilled within its own pages. Notably, Jesus foretells his rejection, death and resurrection (e.g., Mk 8:31). And it happens. Yet strangely, it is strikingly hard to give an example of such fulfillment *between* the Testaments. Matthew 1–4, for instance, refers seven times to fulfillment, but none of the references involve the kind of direct relationship with the quoted prophecies that appears in those fulfillments within the First Testament and within the New Testament. When Jews argue with Christians about whether Jesus is the Messiah, they point out that the Christian claim is implausible because Jesus did not fulfill First Testament hopes. Jesus did not introduce a lasting reign of God's righteousness and justice in the world. They thus see the Christian as "the incomprehensibly daring man who affirms in an unredeemed world that its redemption has been accomplished."[14]

In seeking to understand the theological significance of this phenomenon, I am helped by Paul's comment about Jesus that "whatever promises of God there are, in him there is a 'Yes'" (2 Cor 1:20). God's promises are not all *fulfilled* in Christ (in the sense in which we commonly use the word *fulfill*), but they are all *confirmed* in Christ. The fact that Jesus came, healed people, expelled demons, stilled the storm, submitted to rejection and execution, rose to new life, and overwhelmed people with God's Spirit is evidence for seeing him as the confirmation of God's promises. Most of these acts are not the *subject* of the promises, but they do back them up. They indicate that God was at work in Jesus and that this activity of God's is one with the promises God made through the prophets. We don't exactly need the New Testament in order to make it possible for us to believe in God's promises; at least, many Jews believe in them without believing in Jesus. But the New Testament does direct us back to the First Testament to discover the promises there that we can believe in.

---

[14]Martin Buber, *Israel and the World*, 2nd ed. (New York: Schocken, 1963), p. 40.

SPIRITUALITY

Do we need the New Testament because without it we wouldn't know how to relate to God, know how to pray, know how spirituality works? Jesus begins the Sermon on the Mount with a prophetic summary of the dynamics of life with God (Mt 5:3-11). He tells people that it is all right to be crushed and to be longing for God's righteous purpose to be fulfilled. God is going to respond to that longing. People who are crushed and mourning are in the position out of which people pray in the Psalms, and in response Jesus speaks in the way a prophet might speak to people in that position. Most of the wording in the Beatitudes starts from the Psalms and Isaiah. It's not surprising that Ephesians 5:18-20, in bidding people to be filled with the Spirit, goes on to bid them to speak to one another in psalms and hymns and spiritual songs (cf. Col 3:16). Nor is it surprising that the praise of heaven as Revelation describes it looks very much like the praise of the Psalms.

The same applies to prayer in Revelation; it looks like prayer in the Psalms. In Revelation 6 John sees the martyrs under the altar in heaven (there is an altar in heaven because heaven is the heavenly temple, and a temple has an altar). They are praying in the way people do in the Psalms, crying out and asking how long it is going to be before the Lord judges and takes revenge for their blood from the people on earth. It might seem that the appropriate Christian response to their prayer would be to tell them that because they live after Christ, they ought not to be praying in that way; if it was a way of praying that was tolerable before Christ, it is hardly one that is acceptable any longer. Instead, the Lord gives each of them a white robe and does not rebuke them except by telling them to wait a little longer until the full number of their brothers and sisters has been killed as they have been. "Their petitions for justice and vindication against their oppressors are the postmortem equivalent of the widow's pleas for justice in Luke 18:3, so it is not surprising to read God's similar response."[15] Events later in Revelation constitute the fulfillment of that promise, within the vision. When we were young, we may have been told that God answers prayer by saying yes, no or wait. On this occasion, we might have thought God would answer "no," but actually God gives the other two answers, "Yes, but wait." Apparently it is

---

[15]David Crump, *Knocking on Heaven's Door* (Grand Rapids: Baker, 2006), p. 271.

still okay to pray for one's attackers to be punished (and thus to depend on God to be the one who does something about their attacks).

When Jesus gives the disciples what we call the Lord's Prayer, it might be asked whether he means people are to say these actual words, or whether they are to take the prayer as a pattern. I assume the answer is that it has both significances. The same is true of the Psalms. They are meant for us to pray; they are also a pattern for prayer. The Lord's Prayer is itself an example; it especially recalls Psalm 145.[16] Because "my God" reigns over all, I can address God as "our Father who is in heaven." I urge that God's name be hallowed, that God's reign become a reality, that God's will be done and I ask for bread for each day, for the forgiveness of my wrongdoing, for protection from temptation and for deliverance from evil. All these prayers are in keeping with Psalm 145. The liturgical addition to the Lord's Prayer, "Yours is the reign, the power and the glory, forever and ever," sums up the Psalms. Indeed, Dietrich Bonhoeffer notes that it would not be difficult to arrange all the Psalms under the petitions of the Lord's Prayer.[17]

So the New Testament affirms the ways of worshiping and praying that appear in the First Testament and implicitly draws our attention to them. When Ephesians and Colossians urge people to sing psalms, hymns and spiritual songs, I assume that they include reference to the psalms in the Psalter, but I also assume that they don't confine their reference to them. At the beginning of his Gospel, Luke includes the songs of praise by Mary and Zechariah that I have quoted, which I assume would count as hymns or spiritual songs. Like the praise in Revelation, they constitute praise of a kind one finds in the Psalms, in this case praise that bases itself on what God is now doing afresh. As is appropriate in the context, they thus most resemble thanksgiving psalms—testimony psalms, one may as easily call them. Like such psalms, they recount what God has just done for the person who is praying, go on to reaffirm truths about God that have been newly demonstrated in what God has done, express confidence for the future in light of what God has done, and assume that what God has done for the person who is praying is of signifi-

---

[16]Cf. Erich Zenger, "Dass alles Fleisch den Namen seiner Heiligung segne," *Biblische Zeitschrift* 41 (1997): 1-27; cf. Reinhold G. Kratz, "Die Gnade des tägliche Brots," *Zeitschrift für Theologie und Kirche* 89 (1992): 1-40 (25-28); Goldingay, *Old Testament Theology* (Downers Grove, IL: IVP Academic, 2009), 3:184-85.

[17]See Bonhoeffer, *Life Together/Prayerbook of the Bible* (Minneapolis: Fortress, 1996), pp. 58, 177.

cance for other people; it builds up their faith and hope. Like some examples of this kind of praise in the Psalms, they praise God for having done what God has actually not yet done but has made a commitment to doing; because God has made that commitment, the deed is as good as done.

The nature of the praise and prayer in the Psalms indicates how memory is key to praise and prayer. In praise, people recall what God did in creation, at the exodus and in Israel's subsequent story, and recall that God himself is one who remembers. In prayer they again remember what God has done, but do so with wistfulness and pain, yet also with the intention of prodding God's memory. In thanksgiving they resist the temptation to put out of mind the pain they have just been through and instead insist on telling the story of their affliction, their prayer and God's rescue, in order that this story may become part of their friends' memory, so that they, too, may "remember" this story and may have their trust and hope built up.

Ethics

Memory relates to ethics as well as to spirituality (the distinction between ethics and spirituality is a Western one and does more harm than good). Memory places obligations upon you. The Israelites were to remember their experience of servitude in Egypt, and treat their servants accordingly. But do we need the New Testament because it lays before us a higher ethical ideal than that of the First Testament?

Jesus suggests several hermeneutical clues for understanding the significance of the First Testament in this connection; in chapter eight we will consider them in more detail. One comes in a response to a question about this subject. If you want to understand the Torah and the Prophets, Jesus says, you need to see them as all dependent on the commands in the Torah to love God and love your neighbor (Mt 22:40). Augustine thus declared that the proper test of interpretation is whether it builds up our twofold love of God and our neighbor.[18] The entirety of the Torah and the Prophets is an outworking of those two commands. It may be hard for us to see the Torah and the Prophets that way, when we read of Moses laying down a puzzling rule about not boiling a kid goat in its mother's milk (and doing so three

---

[18]See *On Christian Doctrine* IV.36.

times) or telling the Israelites to slaughter the Canaanites. Yet Jesus sees the
Torah and the Prophets thus, and it is illuminating to keep his twofold principle in mind in reading them. How does this or that command work toward
the twofold love? Conversely, the implication also is, if you want to know
what love is, read the Torah and the Prophets.

A second comment by Jesus helps show why some of those commands are
puzzling. He is again responding to a question. Is divorce permissible, and if
not, why did Moses presuppose that it was? A command like this one, Jesus
says, was given because of people's hardness of hearts, even though it doesn't
 fit with God's creation intent (Mt 19:8). One can see how Moses' command is
an expression of love. Given that we fail to live up to God's creation intention,
it wouldn't be an act of love for God then simply to say, "Well, you're on your
own now." In particular, in a patriarchal society, when a woman has been
thrown out by her husband, it wouldn't be an act of love to leave her without
any documentation of her marital status. So the Torah requires that she be
given such documentation. In this connection, the Torah thus starts where
people are in their sinfulness. The New Testament does the same. Although
the First Testament talks about slavery, Middle Eastern slavery was not an
inherently oppressive institution like the European slavery accepted under the
Roman Empire and then accepted by Britain and the United States. It would
be better to call Middle Eastern slavery "servitude," a servitude that could
provide people who become impoverished with an economic safety net. The
Torah accepts such servitude but places constraints on it, such as limiting its
length to seven years and requiring that a servant be treated as a member of
the family. The New Testament does urge masters not to ill-treat their slaves,
but otherwise it shrugs its shoulders at this aspect of human hardness of heart.

A third comment by Jesus comes at the beginning of Matthew, though I
refer to it last because it's harder to interpret. Jesus comes not to annul the
Torah or the Prophets but to fulfill them (Mt 5:17). Elsewhere in the New
Testament "fulfilling" the law commonly means obeying it, and Jesus does
embody in his life the expectations of the Torah and the Prophets. He also
"fulfills" the hopes of the Torah and the Prophets. Yet what he goes on to say
in Matthew 5 points in another direction. While English translations use the
technical-sounding word *fulfill*, the word Matthew uses is also the ordinary
Greek word for *fill*. We have noted that when the New Testament talks about

fulfilling prophecy, it doesn't mean that the event in question simply corresponds to the prophecy. In effect it means something more like filling out or filling up. In Matthew 5 it makes sense to think of Jesus filling out the expectations of the Torah and the Prophets, working out their implications.

The command about loving enemies provides a convenient example. "You have heard it said, 'Love your neighbor and hate your enemy'" (Mt 5:43). Now there is no command or exhortation to hate your enemy in the First Testament or in Jewish teaching from Jesus' day.[19] There are of course expressions of hatred toward enemies in the Torah and the Prophets; but then, there are examples in the New Testament. Jesus himself tells people to hate their family (Lk 14:26), whereas the First Testament never tells people to hate anyone. Indeed, Jesus is the only person in the Bible who tells people to hate other people. Loving your neighbor in the First Testament is the equivalent of loving one another in the New Testament (e.g., Jn 13:34; Rom 13:8; 1 Pet 1:22; 1 Jn 3:11).[20]

Further, the First Testament gives examples of people loving their enemies, and when it tells people to love their neighbor (Lev 19:18), the context makes clear that the neighbor they are being bidden to love is the neighbor who is their enemy (people hardly need to be told to love the neighbor they get on with). So Jesus is making explicit something implicit in the commandment. Thus other Jewish teachers in Jesus' day could have accepted his teaching on the subject, as an exposition of the Scriptures. There was nothing shocking about it. One could say he is fulfilling or filling out or filling up the Torah by making explicit what the command implies, as well as by obeying it.

Jesus does put radical demands before people, but so did Isaiah and so does Proverbs. The New Testament is new in the same way that Isaiah was new or that Genesis was new over against Exodus.[21] While there are statements Jesus makes that no prophet or wise teacher could have made, these

---

[19]Christian scholars refer to passages such as the Qumran *Hymns* XIV and *Manual of Discipline* I.9-11; IX.15-22 (see, e.g., Allen Verhey, *The Great Reversal* [Grand Rapids: Eerdmans, 1984], p. 144; Eduard Lohse, *Theological Ethics of the New Testament* [Minneapolis: Fortress, 1991], p. 57; Richard A. Burridge, *Imitating Jesus* [Grand Rapids: Eerdmans, 2007], p. 329), but these passages focus on repudiating God's enemies, not the community's enemies, and their language and stance compare with ones that appear in the New Testament (e.g., 2 Thess 1:5-9).

[20]Leslie C. Allen, *A Theological Approach to the Old Testament* (Eugene, OR: Wipf and Stock, 2014), p. 70.

[21]Cf. R. Walter L. Moberly, *The Old Testament of the Old Testament* (Minneapolis: Fortress, 1992).

are statements such as the "I am" declarations in John's Gospel; they relate
to his being the incarnate one and the Savior. He puts radical demands
before people because he is a prophet and because he is the embodiment of
wisdom and because he is the embodiment of God's grace and truth. What
he said could have scandalized people, but not because it went against what
the First Testament said or because they could not have found it in the First
Testament if they had looked with open hearts.

Yes, of course, we need the New Testament Scriptures, but they don't
supersede the earlier Scriptures. We need the First Testament for an under-

standing of the story of God's working out his purpose, for its theology, for
its spirituality, for its hope, for its understanding of mission, for its understanding of salvation and for its ethics. The following chapters will develop
aspects of these points, sometimes directly taking up points that I have pre-
viewed in this first chapter.

2

Why Is Jesus Important?

We need the New Testament because it tells the story of Jesus, and this story is of crucial importance. Why is that so? What does the New Testament tell us about Jesus' significance?

The introduction to each Gospel declares that Jesus came to bring the fulfillment of God's purpose for Israel as his people. In Matthew he comes as the climax of the three-act drama extending from Abraham to David, from David to the exile and from the exile to his appearance (Mt 1:1-17). As a descendant of David and Abraham, he is eligible to be the Anointed One (the Messiah, the Christ) and he is set in the context of God's purpose to bless the nations. Like the prophet who speaks in Isaiah 52:7-10, he declares that God's reign has come: as Babylon reigned over Israel earlier, more recently Rome has been reigning, but that reign is now being terminated.

Mark gets more briskly into an account of Jesus' proclamation that "God's reign has come near" (Mk 1:15). The signs of this fact are Jesus' expelling impure spirits from people, healing them, cleansing them, declaring their forgiveness and associating with people who earn their money from dubious occupations. In due course he chooses twelve of his followers and sends them off to issue his proclamation and to expel impure spirits themselves (Mk 3:13-19). Jesus meets with varying forms of response—curiosity, commitment, skepticism and also opposition from many scholars, from many people who see themselves as dedicated to living by the Scriptures, and from many people with religious or political responsibility.

In Luke's account of the way Jesus brings the fulfillment of God's purpose for Israel, he takes up the proclamation to the poor in Isaiah 61 (see Lk 4:16-21).

In Isaiah 61, the poor are not the people within a community who lack resources, but the community as a whole whose life is hard as it lives under the dominion of a foreign power. In Jesus' context, Israel's position is the same, and as the objects of preaching and teaching, the term *the poor* has this broader meaning in Luke. It denotes the people as a whole. With this connotation, Jesus' quotation from Isaiah fits Luke's opening account of the significance of his coming (Lk 1:46-79). Jesus' disciples are not people lacking resources, but they are poor because they belong to this people under the oppressive and demoralizing dominion of a foreign power (e.g., Lk 6:20). They are indeed thus poor in spirit (Mt 5:3). Jesus does not focus on a concern for the poor in the sense of people who lacked resources.

In John, Jesus' coming has its background in the rejection of God's message by the world in general and by his own people. So he comes to bring them grace and truth. John takes up the way Yahweh had revealed himself as the God who is full of grace and truth (Ex 34:6-7). Moses declared it to be so and the Torah expresses the fact, but by their nature neither Moses nor the Torah could embody or incarnate the fact. Jesus has done so. No one had seen God in that sense. Jesus has now made him known. Yahweh's grace and truth have come through Jesus: "Out of his fullness we have all received grace in place of grace already given" (Jn 1:16, TNIV).

In none of the Gospels does Jesus tell his disciples to extend the kingdom, work for the kingdom, build up the kingdom, or further the kingdom.

What Jesus Did and What He Was

When John the Baptizer receives reports in prison of what Jesus was doing, he sends to ask whether Jesus is "the one who is to come," the expected Messiah. Maybe John is implicitly affirming that Jesus is the fulfillment of such hopes; maybe he has doubts. Jesus points to his acts of healing, cleansing, resuscitation and preaching to the poor (Lk 7:18-23). Since these acts do not correspond to the role of "the one who is to come" whose tasks have been described in the songs of Mary and Zechariah (Lk 1:46-79), John can hardly be faulted if he does have doubts. Jesus' acts are more those of a prophet. Thus when Peter declares that Jesus is the Anointed One (Mt 16:16-27), Jesus blesses him, yet also tells him not to talk in these terms to people. Jesus is destined to be killed, but then to come back to life. His fate follows from the strange fact that his own people will end up repudiating him and killing him, as happened with the prophets.

Jesus focuses his ministry on his own people, though he occasionally heals Gentiles (e.g., Mt 8:5-13), and on one such occasion contrasts a centurion's faith with that of Jews. In light of this contrast, he declares that the people who belong to God's reign will be thrown out of it; cursing a fig tree because it is producing no fruit is an enacted prophetic sign of this dismissal (see Mt 20–22). Set in the context of the First Testament, however, Jesus' vocation to bring good news to Israel is also a vocation to bring about blessing for the world, in keeping with God's promise to Abraham. In John, likewise, he comes to take away the world's sin (Jn 1:29). He is the Savior of the world (Jn 4:42). In light of his coming, arguments about the right mountain for worship will become irrelevant; people will worship in spirit and truth (Jn 4:21-24). He has other sheep beyond the ones in Israel's pen; there is to be one flock, one shepherd (Jn 10:16). He dies for the Jewish nation and for God's scattered children (Jn 11:51-52). Some Greeks seek to see him, and he comments that he is going to draw all people when he is lifted up (Jn 12:20, 32).

Looking at Jesus and listening to him might make people think of Moses (teaching and feeding), of Elijah and Elisha (doing miracles and gathering a group of disciples), of a priest (forgiving sins, making declarations about purity or the Sabbath), of a prophet (speaking God's word, but experiencing persecution and martyrdom), of the Anointed One for whom Israel hoped (bringing God's reign), and of the "human figure," the "Man" or "Son of Man" in Daniel (having authority to judge). Exorcizing, healing, calming storms, walking across a lake and creating food to feed huge crowds were signs of supernatural power, though such power had been exercised by Moses, Elijah and Elisha. He came from God, and his teaching and authority came from God, but those facts indicated only that he was a prophet, or the Anointed One. He is the light of the world (Jn 8:12); but so are his disciples (Mt 5:14).

Although he was like such First Testament figures, then, one could understand him only if one combined them (cf. Mk 1:11; 9:7; Heb 1:1). He was like them, only more so. Moses and Elijah appear with him, but he is the one his disciples are to heed (Mk 9:2-7). He is way more significant than Moses (Heb 3:1-6). "All things have been committed to me by my Father," he says; he alone knows the Father and reveals him (Mt 11:27). Before Abraham was born, "I am" (Jn 8:58). He is the resurrection and the life, and he gives eternal life; he is in the Father and the Father is in him; he is the only way to the Father (Jn 10:28; 11:25; 14:6, 10). While the Torah had been given through Moses, grace and truth came through Jesus (Jn 1:17-18); we have noted that grace and truth are proclaimed in the Torah, all right, but in Jesus they are embodied in a person. He is the very image of the invisible God (Col 1:15). So the only appropriate response to him is to bow down and say, "My Lord and my God" (Jn 20:28).

WHAT JESUS SAID

As a prophet and a teacher (e.g., Mt 8:19; 13:57; Lk 24:19; Jn 13:13), Jesus is an interpreter of the Scriptures (e.g., Mt 7:12), and his teaching corresponds to the teaching of the First Testament. Like the Torah, he looks for a community characterized by generosity in giving, lending and forgiving.[1] As First Testament prophets undermine the idea that God wants people to offer sacrifices, Jesus undermines the idea that there is any point in rules about purity (Mk 7:1-23). Like a First Testament prophet, he can push people to accept more radical standards from within the Torah than the Torah sometimes allows—for instance, in forgoing the right to divorce your wife (Mk 10). Like a First Testament figure such as Job, he can push people to examine their attitudes as well as their actions (see Job 31). Like the First Testament teachers whose work appears in Proverbs, he can urge people to be peacemakers, but can also be realistic about the fact that there are always going to be wars (Mt 5:9; 24:6-7). Indeed, he comes to bring a sword, not to bring peace—to set family members against each other because of the different way they will respond to him (Mt 10:34). In keeping with stories in books such as Judges and Samuel–Kings, he also declares that people who draw the sword die by the sword (Mt 26:50-54).

What is distinctive and engaging about Jesus is not the novel things he says but the way he says things. He is creative not so much because he says things that are completely new but because he speaks with such authority. "All he says and does is transparent, crystal-clear, and self-evident."[2] At the same

---

[1]If Jesus was proclaiming the implementation of the jubilee year (e.g., John H. Yoder, *The Politics of Jesus*, 2nd ed. [Grand Rapids: Eerdmans, 1994], pp. 60-75), it is an example of this urging the implementing of the Torah, in light of the distinctive socioeconomic situation of his context.

[2]Leonardo Boff, *Jesucristo y la liberación del hombre* (Madrid: Cristiandad, 1981), p. 122; cf. Jon Sobrino, *Jesus the Liberator* (Maryknoll, NY: Orbis, 1993), p. 158.

time he is controversial, not least in what he says about God, because he says things that people ought to recognize but that they avoid: such as God's prioritizing life, mercy and reconciliation over rules, religious tradition, learning and acquiring stuff, especially when the latter clash with those priorities.[3]

He has some distinctive teaching over against the Prophets and Proverbs. We have noted that hell is a distinctive motif in his teaching; all but one of the New Testament references to hell come on his lips. People who call other people "fools" are in danger of hell's fire, so they are to be afraid of the one who can destroy both body and soul in hell (Mt 5:22; 10:28; see also Mt 5:29-30). Fiery judgment is a recurrent theme in his teaching (e.g., Mt 11:20-24; 13:41-42, 49-50)—much more prominent than exhortations to love one's enemies or to be peacemakers. He speaks much of eternal punishment (e.g., Mt 25:31-45). He emphasizes the conditionality of forgiveness: speaking against the Holy Spirit will not be forgiven, and neither will failure to forgive others (Mt 12:32; 18:35). He will disown people who disown him (Mt 10:33).

By no means is it the case, then, that Jesus stands for unconditional forgiveness or love (over against the God of the First Testament's standing for wrath). Yet he did not come to judge but to save (Jn 12:47), and another distinctive theme over against the Torah and the Prophets is resurrection and eternal life (e.g., Mt 22:23-33). People who believe in Jesus will find that they have a spring of water welling up to eternal life (Jn 4:14; cf. Jn 6:27, and much of Jn 6). Both aspects of eternal destiny are prominent in John (e.g., Jn 3:15-17, 36). God has entrusted the judgment of the world to him; people will rise to live or to be condemned (Jn 5:22-29).

While the Gospels refer frequently to Jesus' activity in teaching and speak much of his speaking about who he is, they give less space than one might expect to his teaching on matters such as God's expectations of us. We have less of Jesus' teaching on such themes than we have from (say) Jeremiah, or from Paul, who is the New Testament's great teacher and prophet concerning the faith and life of a congregation and the distinctiveness of the life of a disciple. It seems that Jesus' job was to act, and Paul's job was to interpret his acts. Outside of what he has to say about himself, he doesn't give much distinctive teaching except those warnings about hell and about the possi-

---

[3]Cf. Sobrino, *Jesus the Liberator*, pp. 160-79.

bility of never being forgiven. "It wasn't by argument that it pleased God to save his people."[4] They had plenty of teaching in the Scriptures. Their problem was that they weren't getting it. They needed something new to be done for and about them.

What Happened to Him

In the second half of Jesus' story, exorcism and other signs give way to letting himself be martyred. While it is a strange contrast, it is the logical outcome of the response he has met, especially from those with power among his people. It is in keeping with the way people had often treated prophets. It is also in keeping with a picture that emerges from the First Testament, especially from the visions in Daniel that speak of a coming time of wrath and unprecedented trouble, but then of restoration (e.g., Dan 8:19; 11:36; 12:1-3). Daniel 9 further associates Jerusalem's continuing desolation with its waywardness and thus speaks of a time when its sin will be expiated, but also of the putting to death of an anointed one. The visions refer directly to the persecution of faithful Jews by Antiochus Epiphanes, but the community's suffering in Antiochus's day continued the experience begun under Babylon and continues in its subjugation to Rome. These motifs became important in other Second Temple writings that form the background to Jewish thinking in Jesus' day, and it is not much of a leap to see the Anointed One's submitting himself to death as the means whereby forgiveness and restoration would come.[5]

One can thus imagine Jesus' submitting to death on the basis that it would have this fruit, and see it as accompanied by a conviction that death would not be the end for him; he would come back from the dead (e.g., Mt 16:13-27). This confidence did not take away from the terror of dying and of being abandoned by the Father who could rescue him (Mt 27:46). The rescue did come, but in the form of raising him from death. He then departed to be with God, but poured out his spirit on his followers. In the first public declaration about him after this event, Peter gives an account of his story that embraces signs, execution, resurrection, ascension and outpouring (Acts 2:22-36). It is the story he and other followers can keep telling because they have been the

---

[4]Ambrose of Milan, *Exposition of the Christian Faith* I:5 (I:42); cf. Karl Barth, *Church Dogmatics* I, 1 (Edinburgh: T & T Clark, 1956), p. 88.
[5]See Brant Pitre, *Jesus, Tribulation, and the End of the Exile* (Grand Rapids: Baker, 2005).

witnesses of these events (cf. Acts 1:8; 3:15; 5:32; 10:39, 41; 1 Pet 5:1).

With hindsight and the recollection of some prompting by Jesus, these followers can see that the execution had to happen (Acts 4:28). It fitted the Scriptures (Acts 2:23; 3:18). Paradoxically, the very fact that Jews and Gentiles conspired to kill him (cf. Acts 4:27) showed why it had to happen. The story of humanity and the story of Israel are the story of people resisting God and seeking to exclude God from his world (cf. Jn 1:1-12). But "'the hidden counsel of God' . . . worked also through Caiaphas and Pilate."[6] The story of humanity and the story of Israel are also the story of God's insisting on staying with humanity and with Israel, chastising them but never letting them go. They are the story of God's sacrificing himself for the world and for Israel. So the logical terminus of the story is of God letting humanity kill him, but then of his rising from death in order to prove that even that act can defeat neither the love nor the power of God. Jesus' death and resurrection thus constitute the defeat of evil and the guarantee that God's purpose for humanity and for Israel will find fulfillment.

Jesus' death and resurrection mean that the way into the presence of God and to resurrection life is open. When Jesus dies, the temple curtain tears and dead bodies rise (Mt 27:51-53; cf. Heb 8:8; 9:15; 10:19). Jesus' death is the ultimate expression of God's faithful commitment to Israel and the world. It is consistent with the way he had been leaving sin unpunished over the centuries. Whereas our unfaithfulness made us deserving of judgment, Jesus' faithfulness more than counterbalanced our unfaithfulness. It can count for us if we associate ourselves with him (Rom 3:21-26). Jesus' death embodied God's willingness to take responsibility for people's wrongdoing even though they did not deserve it, and therefore to forgive them rather than hold their sins against them. It was thus the act whereby God put right his relationship with the world and with Israel, which had become broken (Rom 5:11). It was an act of expiation whereby God cleansed humanity and Israel from the taboo attaching to them, which would have made it impossible for God to associate with them (Rom 3:24). It was an offering that the Father could receive from the Son as priest, to make reparation for the history of waywardness that had characterized Israel and the world (Heb

---

[6]Oliver O'Donovan, *The Desire of Nations* (Cambridge: Cambridge University Press, 1996), pp. 121-22.

5–10). Like a president pardoning people, God pardoned the world, defeating the supernatural powers that insisted that the charges that could be brought against people should be the basis for keeping them in a situation of guilt (Col 2:13-15). What he achieved through accepting execution applies to these people, too; in effect, they were also executed. It was thus an act of redemption because it freed humanity and Israel from being locked into waywardness (1 Pet 1:18-19).

What Follows

After his death and resurrection, Jesus' followers ask whether the time has arrived when Jesus will restore sovereignty to Israel. During his ministry Jesus had declared that God's reign was arriving. Did that declaration mean Israel would now be free of Roman authority and could live under God's sovereignty? Now that he is raised from the dead, has the moment come? It's not for you to know the date, he says. It will happen, but they may not know when it will happen. Instead, they are to receive power to tell the world about him. And he will come back (Acts 1:6-10). Surprisingly (or not), their experience as they begin giving their witness is the same as Jesus' experience; most of his own people don't want to know. On the other hand, many Gentiles do. So the proclamation of Jesus gets diverted from his own people to focus on the Gentiles.

Paul later sees this development as the implementation of the purpose God had long intended (see Rom 9–11). Bringing the gospel to the Gentiles thus has a prominent place in his letters, which are all addressed to congregations of largely Gentile believers. The people of God is now living in different situations than the ones the First Testament Scriptures mostly address, when whole communities (cities or villages) were part of the people of God. But Israelites had also sometimes lived as alien groups in foreign countries, which was initially the situation of the groups of people who believed in Jesus. Over subsequent centuries, congregations often continued to be groups whose faith made them aliens, though sometimes their situation matched that situation within the First Testament, and a village or a city would be "Christian."

Meanwhile, for the life of congregations around the Mediterranean, the New Testament works out the implications of the First Testament's vision as it has been "fulfilled" by Jesus and prescribed by him for life in Judea. "Political theology" is thus articulated in the life of the church: it "takes the church seriously as a society and shows how the rule of God is realized there."[7] In other words, the church's job is to *be* prophetic in its lifestyle. And in this connection the beginning of Acts gives an encouraging portrait of the life of the early Jerusalem church, with its worship, witness, mutual sharing and signs. In accordance with the pattern of Jesus' lifetime, his followers healed, exorcized and raised from the dead; some accepted martyrdom or experienced deliverance from oppressive powers. But things soon start going wrong: there was also deceit, divine judgment, mutual complaint, dispute and argument (e.g., Acts 4:32–5:16). The rest of the New Testament describes churches as having the same double profile.

The New Testament often draws a sharp contrast between how things are as a result of Jesus' coming and how things were beforehand. Paul declares that the result of God's giving Israel the Torah through Moses was to bring death, but Jesus' coming meant that people could see God's glory in Jesus' face, and we are being transformed into the Lord's image with ever-increasing glory (2 Cor 3:7-18). Yet the letters to the Corinthians make clear that much of the congregation's life is not so different from the way of life that the Torah condemns, so that its members risk the same fate as overcame people in Moses' day (1 Cor 10:1-13). Conversely, the First Testament makes clear that there were some people in Israel who enjoyed true life and were reflecting God's glory; the New Testament assumes the point, in the way it describes them in a passage such as Hebrews 11. But Paul's talk about the Torah bringing death reflects the fact that God's covenant relationship with Israel had issued only in death for him until Jesus appeared to him, and the same applied to the Jewish people as a body. Jesus' coming, his death and his resurrection did something revolutionary for the Jewish people, and also did something revolutionary for the Gentile world, on which Paul focuses. Yet the lives of many people in the First Testament show that this transformation was not wholly new, and the life of many people in the New Testament show that it was not effective for all believers in Jesus.

---

[7]Ibid., p. 123.

The Change He Brought

The most distinctive feature of the situation after Jesus came is that the Spirit drove people like Paul to traverse the world to tell the story of Jesus among other nations.

In Western culture "free will" is a fundamental value, and in the introduction to this book I noted that one contrast people draw between the Testaments involves setting the idea of a chosen people based on their choice over against a chosen people based on ethnicity. Like other contrasts between the Testaments, this one oversimplifies or confuses the difference. In the First Testament, to belong to ethnic Israel was neither necessary nor sufficient to a full relationship with God. The story of Israel's capture of Jericho and its aftermath in Joshua 2–7 illustrates the point neatly. Rahab manifests the faith expected of an Israelite and gets adopted into the community; Akan behaves like a Canaanite and gets executed.[8] Israelites had to choose to commit themselves to Yahweh, and Canaanites could do so. Further, Paul's own story shows that God did not abandon ethnic Israel for a people based on their choice. Jesus chooses him—he does not choose Jesus (Jesus gave him no real choice); and Jesus chooses him as an ethnic Israelite.

Closely associated with its account of Jesus' taking hold of Paul, Acts gives an account of the way the Spirit indeed initiates the proclaiming of Jesus' story among the nations. It involves a change in God's missional strategy. That strategy had been to keep Israel distinctive so that it might shine out to the world as his special people and attract people to it. The strategy had achieved some success over preceding centuries. It was supported by the Torah's rules about things that were taboo and things that were clean, which marked Israel out. Now God intends to be more assertive in reaching out to the world, and in this connection the rules about taboo become a hindrance rather than a help. So God abandons them. Potentially, the people of God is now one new humanity embracing Jew and Gentile (cf. Eph 1–3), though in practice it becomes mostly a Gentile church.

What difference did Jesus' coming make to the world? It has been argued that "The Church has made more changes on earth for good than any other movements of force in history," including the growth of hospitals, universities,

---

[8]See Dan Hawk, *Every Promise Fulfilled: Contesting Plots in Joshua* (Louisville: Westminster John Knox, 1991).

literacy and education, capitalism and free enterprise, representative government, separation of political powers, civil liberty, the abolition of slavery, modern science, the discovery of the Americas, the elevation of women, the civilizing of primitive cultures, and the setting of languages to writing.[9] It is easy to dispute this claim. The church resisted some of the developments just listed, some are not particularly Christian, and all were encouraged by humanistic forces and reflect Greek thinking as much as gospel thinking.[10]

One can alternatively do another thought experiment. Imagine we were still waiting for the Messiah, that the first coming of Jesus has not yet happened. How would things in the twenty-first century be different from what they are? In the twenty-first century world there is (among other things) much war, oppression, family dysfunction, marital unfaithfulness and divorce, sexual exploitation and sexual slavery, and economic slavery. It is difficult to claim that the world is in better shape than it was two thousand years ago. I am not clear that the coming of Jesus made much difference to these aspects of how the world is. That fact does not mean Jesus has failed to have the effect he said he would have. He said nothing about the world getting better in these ways. Indeed, he said they would continue the way they were and if anything get worse. Abolitionist Theodore Parker declared his faith that the arc of the moral universe "bends towards justice,"[11] and Martin Luther King and Barack Obama have repeated his conviction. It's sometimes possible to see evidence of that fact in the short term, but I am not clear that there is evidence to justify Parker's faith when one looks at history more broadly. After all, in the nineteenth and twentieth centuries African Americans indeed gained freedom and civil rights, but they needed to do so only because their ancestors had had them taken away, and fifty years after Martin Luther King matters look less encouraging to some African Americans than they did thirty or forty years ago.

The difference Jesus' coming brought about is that there are billions of people in the world who acknowledge the God and Father of our Lord Jesus Christ who would likely not otherwise have done so. This fact is in keeping

---

[9]So D. James Kennedy and Jerry Newcombe, *What If Jesus Had Never Been Born*, rev. ed. (Nashville: Nelson, 2001); quotation from p. 3.

[10]On slavery in particular, see (even when one allows for some overstatement) Hector Avalos, *Slavery, Abolitionism, and the Ethics of Biblical Scholarship* (Sheffield: Sheffield Phoenix, 2011).

[11]*Ten Sermons of Religion*, in *The Collected Works of Theodore Parker* (London: Trübner, 1879), 2:48.

with a New Testament emphasis. It is also the case that when these people die, they have a basis for knowing that they will rise from death on resurrection day, because Jesus' death and resurrection initiated the bringing into being of a resurrected people to which they will belong. The result of Jesus' coming was the preaching of the gospel to the world and the providing of the basis for a confident expectation of resurrection.

What Remains to Be Done

We have noted that Jesus was not the first person in Israel to declare that God's reign had begun. At the Red Sea, when God took on the power of Egypt, Israel had sung, "Yahweh will reign forever and ever" (Ex 15:18). On the eve of the downfall of Babylon, messengers proclaimed to Zion, "Your God has begun to reign" (Is 52:7). Jesus' declaration of God's reign resembled the declaration of God's reign in Isaiah 52. All three declarations belonged in the context of assertions of God's sovereignty in Israel's life but did not meet with the kind of response from Israel that one would have hoped, and the results of the sovereign actions fell far short of what one might have expected. The consummation of God's purpose did not happen. First Testament Israel thus continued to look forward to that consummation. So does the church.

Jesus himself looks forward to a final appearing as judge. After his first declarations about suffering, rejection, death and resurrection, he warns that if a person is ashamed of him and his words, "the Man will be ashamed of him when he comes in his Father's splendor with his holy angels" (Mk 8:38). He speaks further about this appearing in answering a question about the destruction of the temple: "People will see the Man coming in clouds with great power and splendor. Then he will send his aides and gather the chosen from the four winds, from the end of the earth to the end of heaven" (Mk 13:26-27). Paul describes the conversion of the Gentile Thessalonians in these terms: "You turned to God from idols to serve the living and true God and to wait for his Son from the heavens, whom he raised from the dead— Jesus, who delivers us from the coming wrath" (1 Thess 1:9). He later expands on the significance of this event, to which he applies the First Testament term *the day of the Lord*; it will be a day of destruction, but for the Thessalonians a day of salvation from the destruction (1 Thess 5:2-9). At present they are experiencing persecution, but God will pay back affliction to the people who afflict you . . . at the revealing of the Lord Jesus from heaven with his powerful aides, in flaming fire, giving punishment to the people who do not acknowledge God and do not heed the gospel of our Lord, Jesus. They will suffer the punishment of eternal destruction, away from the face of the Lord and from his mighty splendor. (2 Thess 1:6-9)

Revelation gives a much more detailed and vivid description of these events. Paul's own description elsewhere is less vivid, but he regularly refers to the reality of Jesus' appearing as key to the church's faith. In Romans he speaks a number of times about wrath and salvation from wrath (e.g., Rom 5:8-11), but also about the eternal life that will follow for people who have responded to the gospel, about the redemption of their bodies, and about creation itself reaching its destiny (Rom 8). As Peter expresses it in his second sermon, heaven has received Jesus "until the time for the restoring of all things, of which God spoke through the mouth of his holy prophets of old" (Acts 3:21; see further 1 Cor 1:7-8; 15:1-58; 2 Cor 4:16–5:10; Col 1:5; 1 Pet 1:3-13).

To put it another way, God's reign really is going to come (e.g., Acts 14:22; 2 Tim 4:1). As I have studied through the Epistles again in connection with writing this book, one feature that has especially struck me is its emphasis on Jesus' final appearing and on the new life it will usher in for us. It is the job of Paul and others to testify to the coming of God's reign, and he has fellow workers in this connection (Acts 8:12; 19:8; 20:25; Col 4:11). The coming of God's reign will include the restoration of God's reign to Israel, which one might also describe in terms of all Israel being saved, when the deliverer turns impiety from Jacob and brings them forgiveness (Rom 11:26-27).

WHAT THEREFORE HAPPENS NOW

Most of the second half of the New Testament is written to largely Gentile churches. It rejoices in what Jesus has achieved through his execution and resurrection, looks forward to his final appearing, when he will bring God's purpose to its consummation, and instructs congregations about what their life should be like as they live between these two events. A few decades after Jesus' death and resurrection and the outpouring of the Holy Spirit, 2 Peter 3 imagines some people asking, "Where is the promise about his coming?" and commenting that things go on as they always have. The appropriate response, it suggests, is to remember that God works to a different time scale from ours and that he is prepared to wait quite a while to allow time for repentance to people like the readers of the letter. They therefore need to give themselves to living holy lives, not least because that commitment will actually speed his coming.

Given that a thousand years is like a day to the Lord, to him the further passing of two thousand years is only like the passing of two days, and the response in 2 Peter remains appropriate. The church's task is to live a holy life (as it was Israel's task) and to continue to spread a knowledge of the gospel around the world.

The church has also given itself to involvement in action for the betterment of the conditions of people's lives, to what is often called a concern for social justice or for peace and justice. That concern is a biblical one, though not really a New Testament one. There may be several reasons why it is not really a New Testament concern. The average believer was not in a position to (say) engage in advocacy for the abolition of slavery. Most believers were just ordinary people—slaves rather than slave owners. Yet some believers were slave owners rather than slaves, and held other positions of power, and a more profound reason why the New Testament does not focus on bringing about justice in the world is that it encourages believers to focus on the appearing of Jesus. Insofar as they were committed to an activity, it was witnessing to Jesus.

Over two or three hundred years, it became evident that one day for God might indeed turn out to last a thousand human years; the question of a way of living in this age therefore regained importance. Further, within the Roman Empire Christian faith became a typical commitment, not a marginal one, to such an extent that the fourth-century Roman emperor, Constantine, was a believer. Whereas people who acknowledged that Jesus is Lord used to risk martyrdom, now the rulers themselves acknowledged that Jesus is Lord. "The church expected the emperor to act like a Christian, and when he failed to do so it claimed the right to censure him."[12] It is not that the millennium has arrived, but the implementing of some biblical values in the world becomes a possibility as well as a necessity. It remained so in Europe for well over a thousand years.

The New Testament's not speaking about social justice makes the First

---

[12]O'Donovan, *The Desire of Nations*, p. 200.

Testament important in this connection, because the First Testament does so, and offers profound and wide-ranging understandings of what social justice means. One aspect of its significance in this connection is that it recognizes that the society in which the people of God will seek to implement this justice is one that remains sinful. It is in fact fortunate that, as Jesus puts it, the Torah is written for people who have stubborn wills. The Torah seeks to pull people toward God's creation intent, but it makes realistic allowance for their stubbornness (e.g., Mt 19:1-12). The empire and every other society remains a mixed entity, which makes the First Testament distinctively useful in this connection.

Further, the First Testament is under no illusion about whether implementing the Torah has the potential to achieve God's purpose for Israel's life. There is no direct link between seeking to restrain injustice in society and the implementing of God's reign. Implementing God's reign is fortunately God's business. We have noted that the New Testament does not talk about human beings furthering or spreading or building up or working for God's reign. Human efforts to achieve social justice are not destined to be successful. "Our responsibility is not to save the world. We are not required to transform This Age."[13] The problem about human society is too deep. As human beings living in God's world, our vocation is to do what we can to restrain disorder in society, in light of what the Scriptures tell us about God's creation purpose, but not to be overly optimistic about what we can do to bring in the kingdom.[14]

In connection with our life in the world, then, do we need the New Testament? From it we get a further articulation of God's creation ideals. Jesus does not need to give us any new truths or to issue new divine expectations in this connection, though he does provide a fresh prophetic articulation of God's truth and God's expectations. More important is the fact that from his story we know how God's self-giving came to a climax in him as he let himself be martyred. We learn how that self-giving issued in the promise of resurrection and eternal life that extends to the whole world. It is what Jesus did that crucially matters. We could not do without that.

---

[13]George E. Ladd, *The Gospel of the Kingdom* (Grand Rapids: Eerdmans, 1959), p. 157.
[14]Chapter eight will take up these issues further.

3

Was the Holy Spirit Present in First Testament Times?[1]

While one feature that struck me afresh in reading through the New Testament in connection with writing this book is its stress on Jesus' future appearing, another such feature is the stress on the presence and activity of the Holy Spirit as a mark of the life of the church. Here is one reference from each of the letters to churches, from Romans to Thessalonians:

- God's love has been poured out into our hearts through the Holy Spirit given to us. (Rom 5:5)

- My message, my preaching was . . . with a demonstration of the Spirit, of power. (1 Cor 2:4)

- God . . . has sealed us and given us a deposit, his Spirit, in our hearts. (2 Cor 1:22)

- Did you receive the Spirit through acting in accordance with the Torah or through listening with faith? (Gal 3:2)

- When you believed, you were sealed with the promised Holy Spirit. (Eph 1:13)

- We are the circumcision, we who worship by the Spirit of God. (Phil 3:3)

- Epaphras . . . made clear to us your love in the Spirit. (Col 1:8)

---

[1]In this chapter I revisit a question I discussed in "Was the Holy Spirit Active in First Testament Times?" in *Key Questions About Christian Faith* (Grand Rapids: Baker, 2010) and in "The Holy Spirit in the OT" at www.fuller.edu/sot/faculty/goldingay under the Theology tab.

- You received the message, in the context of much affliction, with the Holy Spirit's joy. (1 Thess 1:6)

- God chose you as a first installment for salvation through the sanctifying of the Spirit and through believing the truth. (2 Thess 2:13)

The activity of the Holy Spirit was a mark of the churches' life, something perceptible in people's inner experience and in external events. The predictable nature of this feature of the churches' life makes for a contrast with an earlier incident in one of these cities. When Paul arrived at Ephesus for the second time he found some disciples there who told him, "We haven't even heard that there is a Holy Spirit." So Paul put his hands on them, "and the Holy Spirit came on them and they spoke in languages (prophesied)" (Acts 19:1-6).

During the last third of the twentieth century, charismatic renewal brought a new reality of the Holy Spirit in many people's inner experience and in outward events such as healing and speaking in tongues. It had cooled off a little in Britain by the time I left for the United States in 1997. In California I found it stone cold. At a dinner party we fell to discussing this charismatic movement, and one of the guests expressed herself in terms like those of the disciples in Ephesus. She didn't understand about the Holy Spirit. No one ever talked about it. The situation was back to where it was in 1960, and in Paul's time in Ephesus.

Take Not Your Holy Spirit from Me

The first thing my wife and I do each day (after I make tea) is pray the Episcopal morning devotions, which begin with prayers from Psalm 51:

> Open my lips, O Lord,
>   and my mouth shall proclaim your praise.
> Create in me a clean heart, O God,
>   and renew a right spirit within me.
> Cast me not away from your presence
>   and take not your holy Spirit from me.
> Give me the joy of your saving help again
>   and sustain me with your bountiful Spirit.

In the context of the episode from recent church history that I have just described, these prayers make me recall a remark I heard in a discussion on another occasion. Someone commented on how good it is that we need now never fear that God might take his Holy Spirit from us. If that remark is right, are Episcopalians mistaken to pray those prayers? I thought about this question when my wife and I visited Ephesus and Colossae, two of the cities in Turkey to whose churches Paul wrote the letters from which I quoted above. Ephesus is a gigantic city, Colossae a small one. What they have in common is that they are simply ruins. No one lives there; there is no church there. At Ephesus (my wife observed) there was only a multitude of pagans keen to get back to their cruise ships, and at Colossae there were only two friendly dogs. Neither are there Christian communities in the other places in Turkey whose churches are mentioned in the New Testament. Admittedly a footnote to this observation deserves mention. A century ago there still were churches in Turkey, but as a result of the Balkan wars, the First World War and the Turkish war of independence, Christians fled or were forcibly moved from Turkey to Greece, and reciprocally Muslims moved from Greece to Turkey. But broadly the situation of the church in Turkey applies throughout the Eastern Mediterranean. The countries that were the cradle of the Christian faith, where churches once flourished and where most of its leading theologians once worked, have virtually no Christian presence. A footnote to this observation, too, is that the virtual disappearance of the church in Palestine over recent decades issues in part from Western policy in the Middle East. Might God take his Holy Spirit from his church? It sure looks as if God did it in some of these countries.

There is a sense in which God has not taken his Holy Spirit from his church and would not do so (even the Turkish island of Bozcaada still has a tiny community of monks). When we talk about the presence of God's Spirit, we are talking about the aspect of God whereby God's presence and activities are mediated in our world (the monks ring their church bell on Sunday mornings). God the Father is the Creator and Lord who sits in the heavens. God the Son is the one who once came to earth, then returned to the heavens. God the Spirit is the one who mediates the presence of the always-transcendent Father and the presence of the once-earthly Son. He does so objectively in his church, by doing things such as healing people, and also subjectively, by giving us a sense of God's presence. He operates externally to us and among his people and in our own spirits. Indeed, the use of that word *spirit* in relation to us points to the fact that our spirit is the aspect of us that most intrinsically relates to God. Spirit stands for liveliness, dynamism, energy and vigor, and thus stands for God. Had God not breathed his spirit into us, we would have no liveliness, dynamism, energy or vigor. When Western Christians talk about spirituality, we often have in mind something inward, gentle, quiet and reflective; the scriptural talk about the spirit and the spiritual is different.

Promise and Fulfillment

If God had totally withdrawn his Spirit from us, then he would have withdrawn any reality of his presence and activity, and in addition, we would have no sense of his reality. (Whereas we are inclined to equate the reality and the sense of the reality, these are different things—there can be a reality of God's presence and activity whether we feel it or not, and we can have a sense of God's reality and activity but the sense may be false.) As far as I can see, this withdrawal did take place in the Eastern Mediterranean, and it has taken place not quite as radically in the churches in Europe and less so in the United States, though things are moving that way.

There is also some coming and withdrawing and staying that are part of what happens to individual believers. I was inclined to write "part of individual Christian experience," but it is again easy for us to give the word *experience* a mainly subjective significance, so I avoid the word. The person and activity of God's Spirit are objective realities separate from any sense of them that we may have. When Paul speaks about realities such as the Holy Spirit being poured into our hearts or God sealing us with his Spirit or our receiving the Spirit or our worshiping by the Spirit, at one level he is referring to something that is always true. There is a consistency about the involvement of God's spirit with us; God does not withdraw from us. Yet I have sometimes had the experience—whoops, I mean I have had a sense—of being especially enfolded in God's love, of God's love being spectacularly poured into my heart, on some occasion when I especially needed it. And whereas in England I used from time to time to have a message from God for someone or a vision to share with them, it hardly ever happens now. In this sense, God may have withdrawn his Holy Spirit from me. My general sense of God's reality is more steady, consistent and joyful than it was thirty years ago. But if I were to fail to live the proper life of a servant of God (like King Saul), I could hardly complain if God were to withdraw such activity of the Holy Spirit even though that withdrawal needn't mean God had totally broken off our relationship (any more than it need have that meaning in connection with Saul).

A common implicit Christian understanding assumes that whereas the Holy Spirit was not present and active in First Testament times, the Spirit was then poured out in a once-for-all and permanent way at Pentecost. And there has indeed been an underlying reality of the presence of the Holy Spirit in the church throughout the time since Pentecost, but there have also been special outpourings of the Holy Spirit from time to time that issue in extraordinary visible outward events, and the phenomena reported in Acts and reflected in the Epistles look like one of those outpourings that came—and went. Conversely, we will note below that the First Testament does not give the impression that the Spirit of God was not present and active in First Testament times.

Peter sees the day of Pentecost as an indication that "the last days" have come, though evidently there is a straightforward chronological sense in which it is not so. There is nothing novel about the idea that the End had arrived and yet that in another sense the End remained future. The Prophets and Lamentations already knew that the End or Yahweh's Day was arriving or had arrived in their time, yet they also knew that the End remained future—that after the End had in some sense arrived, it still needed to be awaited, and that the people of God had to live in light of what God had done and in light of what God was still to do.

Specifically, Acts 2 sees the outpouring of the Holy Spirit at Pentecost as a fulfillment of a promise in Joel 2:28-32, and one could get the impression that the promise in Joel gets its intended once-for-all fulfillment then. Yet Joel itself does not associate its prophecy with "the last days"; that expression is part of Peter's interpretation of the prophecy. It reflects how New Testament references to First Testament prophecies commonly don't correspond to the prophecies' own meaning. The New Testament uses prophecies to gain an understanding of events in its own day; it is not exegeting the prophecies in order to discover what God was communicating to people when the prophecies were given. The prophecies' inherent meaning is often not important to the New Testament's purpose. So we wouldn't necessarily expect Peter's quotation in Acts 2 to relate to the Joel prophecy's own meaning. Ironically, indeed, the recurring and occasional nature of subsequent outpourings of the Holy Spirit on the church might fit the inherent meaning of the promise in Joel rather better than the common Christian understanding of the prophecy as envisaging a one-time event.

Holy Spirit

Unlike most prophetic books, Joel doesn't give readers the date of the prophet's activity in terms of the reigns of Israelite kings, which may well mean that (like Malachi) it comes from a time when there were no kings. But Joel's message in its context is clear enough even if we don't know the period to which he belongs; it is apparent what kind of situation he is addressing. There has been a natural or military disaster, and the people need to turn to Yahweh. Yahweh promises that he will see off the invaders (locusts or human armies) that have devastated the land and will restore it so that people have something to eat again. But that is not all:

> Afterward, I shall pour my spirit on all flesh,
> and your sons and daughters will prophesy.
> Your elderly will have dreams,
> your youths will see visions.
> I shall also pour my spirit
> on your male and female servants in those days. (Joel 2:28-29 [3:1-2])

In the past, devastation and recovery have been recurrent experiences in Israel; so have divine withdrawal and divine outpouring. On this occasion, too, devastation and withdrawal will not be the end.

It will help our understanding of the significance of the Joel promise if we bear in mind the two First Testament passages where the precise expression *holy spirit* comes. One is Psalm 51, to which I have referred. An odd aspect of this psalm is that it gives a mixed message about its origin. Its introduction refers to the occasion when David committed adultery with Bathsheba and then saw to the killing of her husband. It was certainly an occasion when David needed to pray for God's mercy, as the psalm does, and for God's spirit not to be taken from him as it was taken from Saul. Yet in these circumstances it would be scandalous for David to say that he has sinned against Yahweh *alone*, and in his time it would be odd to pray for Yahweh to do good to Zion and build up Jerusalem's walls, after which sacrifices can be offered (Ps 51:4, 18-19 [6, 20-21]); Zion is not in need of rebuilding, and the temple has not been either built or destroyed. It has been suggested that a Davidic psalm has been adapted to fit the situation of the people as a whole after the downfall of Jerusalem in 587,[2] or that it was composed in the time of Josiah,[3] or that it was written in the exile and given an introduction to invite readers to read it alongside that story about David without necessarily implying that its origin lies there.[4] In the context of Josiah or the exile, it belongs on the lips of the people together as well as on the lips of an individual such as David; the worship of the church often encourages people to use it in this way. Its *I* is then someone who speaks in the company of others, as when we say in a creed "I believe," or when we sing, "Just as I am." So the psalm implies the frightening possibility that God's spirit might be taken from an individual for specific sins, or from a king like David, or from the people of God as whole. It implies that people fear it may happen—an appropriate fear in Josiah's day, or after the fall of Jerusalem.

The word *spirit* comes three times in Psalm 51:10-12 [12-14], opening the second part of each of three lines. They speak of an upright spirit, a holy spirit and a bountiful spirit. They imply that the people of God could usually trust that God's upright, holy, bountiful spirit was in their midst, acting in relation to them in accordance with those qualities. It might even be turning them into people with such qualities. Applied to a leader, they might imply the loss of the "spiritual" capacities required for leadership (see Is 11:1-5).

The expression *holy spirit* is surprising for reasons other than its novelty. We have noted that *spirit* stands for liveliness, dynamism, energy and vigor, and thus for God. *Holy* also stands for God; it denotes God's extraordinary, powerful, majestic, supernatural, divine nature. So *holy spirit* is close to being a tautology. Both words refer to God in God's God-ness. In the New Testament, translations render the phrase with initial uppercase letters, Holy Spirit. In the psalm, translations are amusingly unsure what to do; some have Holy Spirit, some have holy spirit, and some (like the Prayer Book version quoted above) have holy Spirit. Neither Hebrew nor Greek uses uppercase letters in this way, so they don't have the problem or the facility offered by English. In Psalm 51, the rendering "Holy Spirit" usefully makes a link with the New Testament, but

---

[2]So Derek Kidner, *Psalms 1–72* (London: Inter-Varsity, 1973), p. 194.

[3]So Edward R. Dalgish, *Psalm Fifty-One* (Leiden: Brill, 1962).

[4]So Brevard Childs, "Psalm Titles and Midrashic Exegesis," *Journal of Semitic Studies* 16 (1971): 137-50.

it also encourages us to miss the distinctiveness of what the First Testament says, particularly in this psalm. Giving an uppercase *S* to the middle occurrence of *spirit* separates it from the other two and obscures the parallel between the three occurrences. The psalm is talking about a right, bountiful and holy spirit, and is identifying three characteristics of God's spirit that God needs to make characteristics of Israel's spirit, and not to withdraw it. (Ironically, in this chapter I am myself caught in the same dilemma over the use of uppercase letters; I apologize for the fact that I have not found a way of being consistent about Spirit or spirit, nor for that matter about "he" or "it.")

He Put in the Midst His Holy Spirit

The other occurrence of the phrase *holy spirit* in the First Testament comes in Isaiah 63:7-14, which offers a usefully wide perspective on understanding the activity of God's spirit in Israel.

> I will recount Yahweh's acts of commitment,
> > Yahweh's praises. . . .
> He was the one who restored them, lifted them up,
> > and carried them all the days of old.
> But they—they rebelled
> > and hurt his holy spirit.
> So he turned into their enemy;
> > he himself made war against them.
> But he was mindful of the days of long ago,
> > of Moses, of his people.
> Where is the one who brought them up from the sea,
> > the shepherds of his flock?
> Where is the one who put in its midst
> > his holy spirit,
> the one who made his majestic arm go
> > at Moses' right hand,
> dividing the waters in front of them
> > to make himself a name in perpetuity,
> enabling them to go through the depths like a horse in the wilderness,
> > so they would not collapse,
> like a beast in the vale that goes down,
> > so that Yahweh's spirit would give them rest?

The passage comprises a review of Israel's history that goes back to the beginning. This beginning was a time when God "put in its midst his holy spirit." Haggai 2:4-5 speaks in similar terms: "I am with you (a declaration of Yahweh Armies), the thing that I sealed with you when you got out of Egypt. My spirit remains among you. Don't be afraid." Here, "My spirit is with you" is another way of saying "I am with you." Alas, Isaiah 63 notes, by their rebelliousness Israel "hurt his holy spirit." Yahweh's spirit nevertheless gave them rest in bringing them safely through the Reed Sea (or perhaps in taking them into Canaan: the line can be read either way, and both were true). But the point about this prayer is that Yahweh has now abandoned them. He no longer acts on their behalf in that way.

GOD WITH US, THE SPIRIT WITH US

Whereas Exodus, for instance, talks simply about Yahweh being with Israel or in Israel, Isaiah 63 expresses this reality in terms of God's spirit being with them or in them. One might compare the way Luke 10:20 has Jesus throwing out demons by God's finger, while Matthew 12:28 has him throwing out demons by God's spirit. They are two ways of referring to the same reality. It looks as if Matthew has updated Jesus' words in light of the way the church came to use *spirit* as the normal way to speak about God's activity in the world. The change reflects and corresponds to the way John comments that Jesus' talk about rivers of living water referred to the Spirit, but that he did not talk thus before his "glorification," his death, resurrection and ascension (Jn 7:37-39).

This linguistic phenomenon opens up a broader insight on the First Testament. There, it is explicit that God's spirit is poured out on people from time to time in varying connections. You could thus say that Israel was acquainted with the gifts of the Spirit. Was the Holy Spirit present and active in a more continuous way, so that people produced the fruit of the Spirit such as love, joy and peace? The First Testament certainly tells stories about people who produced that fruit, people such as Abraham and Joseph, Ruth and Hannah—in other words, ordinary men and women, not just people such as kings and prophets. Further, the Psalms comprise the praises and prayers that ordinary people would use, and such praise and prayer is only possible (in New Testament terms) on the part of people who are indwelt by the Holy Spirit. The implication is that the Holy Spirit was indeed present and active in the ordinary lives of Israelites, though they did not often talk in these terms.

It's plausible that Joel, Psalm 51 and Isaiah 63 all belong to the sixth century, or a time a little before or a little after. Their shared use of *spirit* language suggests a linguistic development they shared. These authors, at least, now found it natural to talk about the presence and activity of God in terms of the presence and activity of God's spirit.

The three passages also have in common a context in which Yahweh has turned away his face and abandoned them (as he grants he has in Is 54:7-8), a reality that can also be expressed in terms of withdrawing his spirit. Joel is promising that this withdrawing will not be the end of the story. Perhaps he implies that the failure that had led to the locust plague or military invasion would be bound also to involve the withdrawing of that spirit. The renewing of the land must then also involve the return of God's spirit. We take for granted the image of pouring out God's spirit, but it's not an obvious image, and outside the Joel passage it comes only in Ezekiel 39:29 and Zechariah 12:10. Usually people pour out blood or water, or God pours out wrath; the contrast with that last expression is suggestive. Pouring out does suggest abundance or overwhelming, like the pouring down of rain. In the past, women and men had prophesied, had revelatory dreams and seen visions. In Joel, God promises that it will again become present reality, and the image of pouring suggests that Yahweh will not only restore things by putting his spirit on his people or in their midst, but will pour it out, extravagantly. He will do something more spectacular than they have previously known. Prophecy, dreams and visions will be more prevalent than they have been before. Age, sex, or class will not constrain the pouring out of God's spirit.

In the Roman period, God again seemed to have abandoned his people, and God's coming to them in Jesus thus implied an outpouring of his spirit, a baptizing with his spirit; baptism also implies being engulfed. Those disciples at Ephesus who "haven't even heard that there is a Holy Spirit" hardly mean that they haven't heard of the Holy Spirit. Likewise, when John notes that in Jesus' day "the Spirit was not yet, because Jesus was not yet glorified," he hardly means that the Spirit did not yet exist, though he may reflect the fact that after the glorification there will be a new form of the Spirit's presence as the *paraklētos* who will interpret and bring to mind Jesus' deeds and words. But the verb *is* or *was* in these sentences has the same dynamic implications as apply when Yahweh says, "I am who I am" or "I will be what I will be" (Ex 3:14), or for that matter when the stupid scoundrel says, "There is no god" (e.g., Ps 14:1). It refers to being present, around and active. For the Ephesian disciples, the Holy Spirit belonged to the past or the future, not the present. Paul knows that Jesus has poured out God's spirit and that it can be poured out on them.

While the New Testament sees Joel's promise fulfilled at the first Pentecost, nowadays in many places it is not fulfilled in the life of the church. The sequence of events has followed the one presupposed by Joel. The assumption that God would never withdraw his spirit and therefore cannot have done so implies that what we have now is all there is to have, which is a gloomy view. Joel's promise provides a basis for praying and expecting that the outpouring may happen again.

A RECURRENT PATTERN

I do not imply that either Joel or Acts thought they were announcing an event that was an instantiation of a pattern to be repeated. Prophecy and fulfillment do not work this way. The prophets' task is to tell their own people what God intends to do with them, not to think about what people in hundreds of years' time may need to hear, though the preserving of their prophecies implies the conviction that they have ongoing significance.

Further, the prophets characteristically announce an event that sounds as if it will be the ultimate fulfillment of God's ultimate purpose, and it is characteristic of the New Testament to talk as if that fulfillment has happened. That perspective applies to the verses that follow the promise about God's spirit:

> I shall set portents in the heavens and the earth,
>> blood, fire and columns of smoke.
> The sun will turn to darkness, the moon to blood,
>> before Yahweh's great and awe-inspiring day comes.
> Anyone who calls in Yahweh's name will escape. (Joel 2:30-32)

These declarations look like a description of cataclysmic events at the End, of the kind that are also described in a passage such as Luke 21. Acts 2 sees these declarations, too, as fulfilled at Pentecost, which reflects the fact that Pentecost is itself indeed a partial realization of the End.

Yet it is only a partial realization, as is also characteristic of the fulfillment of prophecy. When a prophet announces the End (with positive or negative implications), we have noted that an end does come, but it turns out not to be *the* End. The indication that Pentecost was not *the* End is the way history continues to unfold, with further withdrawings of the Spirit as well as further outpourings. Given that two thousand more years have passed (three or four times as long as passed from Joel to Pentecost), it seems Pickwickian even to call Pentecost the beginning of the End, though theologically there is a basis for speaking in these terms. It is rather the most magnificent instance of the pattern that runs through the First Testament and continues to run through the church's story, and it is part of the guarantee (as Paul emphasizes) that the End will come. It is also a basis for praying and hoping that we may see more instantiations of the pattern, if we do not see the End itself.

An uncomfortable truth about the Holy Spirit is that we cannot control its coming and operation, as we cannot bring in or further or work for God's reign. We can hurt or grieve the Holy Spirit and forfeit any right to the involvement of God's spirit with us. But in ordinary human experience we cannot make another person fall in love with us or want to spend time with us, and neither can we take action that will ensure that God pours out his spirit on us. Our relationship with God is not contractual, so that we could fulfill the right conditions and it would have the desired results, as if our relationship with God resembled putting coins in a vending machine. It is a personal relationship, and such relationships involve freedom on both sides.

Joel did not speak of an outpouring of God's spirit on the nations, and the people at Pentecost were Jews from abroad, not Gentiles. It is therefore initially astounding when God interrupts Peter's preaching to some Gentiles and pours out the Holy Spirit on them (Acts 10:44-48). Typically, Paul discovers how to think about that reality when he looks at it in light of the Scriptures, like Peter at Pentecost. While the First Testament does not speak of God's spirit being poured out on the nations, it does make clear that Abraham's blessing was intended for the nations. So what is happening is that in Jesus this blessing comes to them as they receive the promise of the Spirit through faith (Gal 3:14). God's giving the Spirit is a fulfillment of his promise of blessing to Abraham. It is another example of the way the First Testament can be referring to the Holy Spirit even when it does not speak in these terms. Paul's words incidentally give us a clue to seeing how people such as Ruth and Hannah could have been producing the fruit of the Spirit: it issued from the fact that they were recipients of the blessing of Abraham. Ruth also provides an anticipatory indication of the promise's application to all the nations.

So do we need the New Testament in connection with an understanding of the Holy Spirit? The usefulness of the New Testament to Jews is that it gives its witness to the fact that God has poured out his spirit on his people in a most dramatic way in the aftermath of performing his ultimate act in Jesus. Israel could know from its Scriptures that God had been giving himself to his people over the centuries and had been involved with them by his spirit over the centuries. Now they know that this self-giving has reached its apogee in Jesus and has received its clearest and most dramatic expression there and at Pentecost. With the right hermeneutic, we Gentiles could have got the point from the First Testament, but the New Testament cuts the corner for us.

Spirit and Torah

In Galatians 3, Paul himself takes the argument about the giving of the Spirit in another direction. He is writing to congregations in Turkey that have known the outpouring of the Spirit of which Joel speaks. Yet some people in those congregations argued that Gentile believers must start obeying requirements of the Torah such as its rules about what one can and cannot eat and about avoiding defilement through contact with people who have themselves been in contact with death. Paul knows that such thinking is confused. With hindsight he can see that living by the Torah had not done him any good. It was through faith that he and they had come to experience the fullness of the Abrahamic blessing, the gift of the Spirit, not through doing things the Torah said.

It was the *must* that was the problem. There were circumstances in which Paul was happy to observe rules in the Torah, in connection with taking and keeping a vow or with circumcision. But the *must* implied that observing the rules in the Torah was the make-or-break factor in a relationship with God. As is the case with any personal relationship, that assumption skews the relationship itself. Trust, not rules, is the basis for relationships. It was the way the relationship between God and Abraham started, and its way of starting announced ahead of time that it would also be the basis of the relationship between God and the Gentile world. First Maccabees 2:52 asks, "Was not Abraham found faithful when tested, 'and it was reckoned to him as righteousness'?" It thereby merges the story of the offering of Isaac in Genesis 22 and the story of his response to God's promise in Genesis 15:6. In Genesis, however, these are two separate events that come in the reverse order, and it is a simple response of trust that means Abraham counts as someone right with God; the offering of Isaac forms a subsequent concrete expression of his submission to God.

At the beginning of its treatment of the Ten Commandments, a rabbinic commentary on Exodus, the *Mekilta* of Rabbi Ishmael, raises the question why the Ten Commandments did not appear at the beginning of the Torah but appear only in the setting of the introductory words that describe Yahweh as the one who brought the people out of Egypt.

> To what may the matter be compared? To one who came to a province. He said to the people, "May I reign over you?" They said to him, "You have done nothing good for us that we should accept your reign." What did he do? He built them a wall. He brought them water. He fought battles for them. Then he said to them, "May I reign over you?" They responded, "Yes! Yes!" Thus it was with God. He redeemed Israel from Egypt. He parted the sea for them. He brought them manna. He provided them a well. He sent them quail. He fought the battles of Amalek for them. Then he said to them, "May I reign over you?" They replied, "Yes! Yes!"[5]

The *Mekilta's* theology is closer to that of Paul and of Genesis in implying that it was not the people's obedience that opened up the possibility of a relationship with Yahweh. Its obedience was a response to Yahweh's acts. In the broader plot line of the Torah as a whole, the promise-trust relationship between God and Abraham came first and even the action-obedience relationship between God and Moses came second. One could thus say that the Torah itself sets obedience in the context of trust. The stance of the people who worry Paul carries the implication (as he sees it) that the rules given centuries after Abraham could undo the promise-trust basis of the rela-

---

[5]Cf. Frederick E. Greenspahn, "Jewish Theologies of Scripture," in *Jewish Bible Theology*, ed. Isaac Kalimi (Winona Lake, IN: Eisenbrauns, 2012), pp. 13-29 (p. 15). Cf. *Mekilta de-Rabbi Ishmael* (Philadelphia: JPS, 1933), 2.229-30.

tionship, as if obedience to the Torah has become the basis of the relationship, instead of trust in Christ. The problem this attitude raises can then be expressed by taking up individual declarations within the Torah, that the person who does the things that the Torah says will live by them and that there is a curse on the person who fails to do what the Torah says. In the Torah, such statements are set in the context of a relationship of trust. The people who worry Paul have compromised that context and treated the rules as if they stood on their own. And if you do try to base the relationship on discrete actions rather than on trust, it is bound to break down. You can never do everything that the agreement lays down.

THE ROLE OF THE TORAH

So why did God give Israel the Torah? Jesus describes it as an exposition of love for God and love for one's neighbor (Mt 22:34-40). Yet Paul is troubled by people who attach the wrong kind of significances to it. The Torah "seems to constitute an enigma in Paul's thought." It is "the instrument of God" but also "the servant of sin." It reveals "God's holy will" so that people may obey it and experience life, but it is also God's means of increasing sin "in order to indict its deadly character."[6] It seems that the Torah was "a calculated risk on God's part."[7] Paul speaks of it having a temporary purpose: it was added to the faith-based relationship God had with Abraham "because of transgressions," until God fulfilled the promise about life that comes through faith in Jesus to both Jews and Gentiles (Gal 3:19). "Because of transgressions" might include the common Jewish idea that it was designed to limit transgression, or the idea that it was designed to deal with transgression by providing the means of gaining cleansing and pardon. Elsewhere, Paul describes it as designed to increase transgression (Rom 5:20), perhaps in the sense that it designated as transgression offenses such as coveting that we might not otherwise have seen as sinful (e.g., Rom 4:15; 5:13; 7:7).

In Galatians 3, he restates his argument by describing the Torah as putting everything under the supervisory control of sin; the Torah was people's custodian or disciplinarian (Gal 3:22, 24). Being such a *paidagōgos* doesn't imply

---

[6]J. Christiaan Beker, *Paul the Apostle* (Philadelphia: Fortress, 1980), p. 235.
[7]James D. G. Dunn, *The Theology of Paul the Apostle* (Grand Rapids: Eerdmans, 1998), p. 159.

being a teacher in a more positive sense;[8] indeed, "pedagogues had the bad image of being rude, rough, and good for no other business."[9] The Torah was people's guardian or trustee or slave-master; both Gentiles and Jews lived under the authority of mere basic religious principles (Gal 4:2-3).[10] The Torah told people, for instance, about what forms of worship they should and should not use and what kind of sanctuary and aids to worship they should and should not have, and about other things they should and should not do, as state law tells people what speed they may drive at or what kind of buildings they may erect, and church law lays down rules concerning worship. More specifically, Paul refers to the observance of days, months, seasons and years (Gal 4:10)—of Sabbath, New Moon, the festivals, the Sabbath Year and so on (cf. Col 2:16). As things would be much worse if we didn't have state law or church law, so things would be much worse without the Torah. While it was a true guide to things God saw as right and wrong, the Torah's function was to perform a kind of holding operation, as is the nature of law. The nature of law qua law is not to get people to love their enemies or avoid coveting but to constrain and limit the effect of the desires that people naturally have and the conflicts between people that arise.

When faith came, the Torah ceased to be in control of people in that way. Thus Jews and Gentiles, men and women, slaves and free people, all relate to God on the same basis in the context of Jesus' coming, on the basis of a response of trust in Jesus as the one who has brought about the fulfillment of God's promise (Gal 3:28). He redeemed people from an obligation to the Torah and thus made it possible for them to move from the position of slaves to the position of (grown-up) sons and daughters. One piece of evidence is the way they call on God as Father, through the presence of Christ's spirit within them (Gal 4:1-7).

UNDER THE LAW AND IN THE SPIRIT

The sequence of law and Spirit reappears in Romans 7–8: the Torah was powerless to enable people to live up to the requirements it laid out, and it thus

---

[8]See Richard N. Longenecker, *Galatians* (Dallas: Word, 1990), pp. 146-48.

[9]Hans Dieter Betz, *Galatians* (Philadelphia: Fortress, 1979), p. 177.

[10]It is a common view that *ta stoicheia tou kosmou* are demonic forces (e.g., Betz, *Galatians*, p. 204); but see (for instance) Bo Reicke, "The Law and This World According to Paul," *Journal of Biblical Literature* 70 (1951): 259-76.

brought only condemnation. Second Corinthians 3 takes the point further. Under the old covenant there was a ministry engraved in letters of stone, a ministry that came with transitory glory but with constraint, and it brought condemnation and death to people whose minds were and are closed. "The law set the standard but offered no power to reach it."[11] Under the new covenant there is a ministry of the Spirit that brings righteousness and life, and comes with surpassing glory and freedom to contemplate it and be transformed (2 Cor 3:7-18). In receiving the Spirit, the Galatians have already experienced the blessing promised through Abraham, which implies the removal of the curses built into the covenant in Deuteronomy; Jesus has borne them (Gal 3:8-14). The fact that the Jewish people ended up under the curse instead of the blessing meant that they could not fulfill their role of being a means of the blessing coming to the Gentiles. In this sense the covenant was actually the main obstacle to the blessing coming to the Gentiles; or at least, continuing observance of the law by Jews who believe in Jesus "was tantamount to evoking the curse of the law on all law-breakers, including the Gentile out-laws."[12]

So is there any significance for the Torah after the Spirit has come, for Jews or Gentiles? Paul might seem to be implying that Jewish believers wouldn't be calling on God as Father if they were still slaves living under a disciplinarian: "As those 'in Christ,' believers experience a more intimate and truly filial relationship with God the Father, one that displaces the legal relationship that existed earlier for God's own."[13] But we have noted that in actuality, people in First Testament times could live in a relationship with God like that of sons and daughters with their father. The stories of people such as Naomi and Hannah show that they had this kind of relationship, as does the prayer life encouraged by the Psalms, and Paul himself implies the point in Romans 9–10. Conversely, the same letters to the Corinthians that speak of believers in Jesus seeing and reflecting God's splendor make clear Paul's recognition that many of the Corinthian believers, at least, did no such thing. The situation in his own day is not so different from what it was in Moses' day or through First Testament times.

Theologically, that fact provides a key reason why the instructions in the Torah continue to be significant for the people of God, Jews and Gentiles.

---

[11]Ralph P. Martin, *2 Corinthians* (Waco, TX: Word, 1986), p. 72.
[12]James D. G. Dunn, *The New Perspective on Paul* (Tübingen: Mohr, 2005), p. 40.
[13]Longenecker, *Galatians*, p. 175.

The implementing of a new covenant (Heb 8–10) has not yet issued in the writing of the Torah into the minds of Christian people in a way that makes it unnecessary for them to teach one another or urge one another to acknowledge God. Paul himself declared that if you love, you will have fulfilled the Torah (Rom 13:8-10), and Augustine urged people, "Love, and do what you will."[14] But the context indicates that Augustine did not mean that an attitude of love somehow guarantees the rightness of what we do, and Paul did not believe that the pouring out of the Spirit made it unnecessary to give instructions to his congregations. We have noted how Jesus described the Torah as an exposition of love for God and love for one's neighbor (Mt 22:34-40). It helps Jews and Gentiles to know what love looks like.[15]

The Reformation stress on justification by faith led to tension about steering a way between the Scylla of legalism and the Charybdis of antinomianism, between the idea that we are right with God on the basis of what we do and the idea that what we do makes no difference to our relationship with God. Often the people who fear legalism should fear antinomianism and the people who fear antinomianism should fear legalism. If Paul had thought in terms of these alternatives, he would have had reason to be more concerned about legalism, and he does not discuss the possible ongoing implications of the Torah as guidance for a life of love. His concern lies elsewhere. In his letters he is confronting concrete situations within congregations, and confronting views people held, and confronting implications of their views. He is acting like a prophet, in fact. In Christian faith there have been people who argued that baptism was essential to salvation or that speaking in tongues was essential to being filled with the Spirit. Such views are analogous to views held in Paul's day, that it was essential that people should be circumcised and keep the scriptural rules about food or Sabbath. People who have held those views about baptism or tongues would not want to imply that we are saved through keeping the Torah, but Paul would see this theology as the implication of their position. He is keen to deny that the Torah can give life; the Torah was not designed to do so (in the sense Paul means), but it is the implication he sees in the position of people who insist that believers observe the Torah.

---

[14]*Homilies on the First Epistle of John* 7 (on 1 John 4:4-12).
[15]See further chapter eight below.

One might make a further link with the following of what are now called religious "practices." That is, someone might say that God requires the observing of certain practices if we are to be in relationship with God at all, to begin taking part in the game. Or someone might say that these practices are key to the ongoing development of a relationship with God, to being able to become more proficient in the game. Paul would be apoplectic about the first view and not very enthusiastic about the second. Both put the emphasis on human action, and risk compromising the fundamental importance of God's grace and our trust. They give us the opportunity to take some initiative in our relationship with God but they also thereby make our initiative the basis of our life with God. They turn something that was key to a holding operation into the reality that the holding operation prepared the way for.

- 4 -

The Grand Narrative and the Middle Narratives in the First Testament and the New Testament

Over recent decades, memory has become a topic of interest in a wide range of disciplines,[1] including biblical studies. As a category for thinking about the past, memory has several advantages over the more traditional term *history*. The word *memory* is an English equivalent to Hebrew and Greek words that come in the Bible, as *history* is not. Remembering is a key imperative in the First Testament, especially in Deuteronomy but also elsewhere. Its significance is taken up by Jesus and by Paul ("Do this in remembrance of me": Lk 22:19; 1 Cor 11:24). Whereas history might seem implicitly to embrace everything, the notion of memory presupposes the selective nature of our relationship with the past, a selectivity based on the significance of the past for the present and the future. While historical study also works in light of the significance of the past for our own concerns, we may present it as otherwise, as totally objective. For better and for worse a focus on memory also subverts some of the inclination to focus on the question whether events happened.

History is inclined to refer especially to the past of a community; we often add an adjective such as *personal* if we use the word to refer to an individual's past. In contrast, in Western culture we are prone to think of memory as an

---

[1]Indeed, Kerwin Lee Klein speaks of "the memory industry" ("On the Emergence of *Memory* in Historical Discourse," *Representations* 69 [2000]: 127-50 [127]).

individual affair, but the Bible assumes that an entity such as Israel has a corporate memory, and modern memory studies emphasize "cultural memory" or "social memory" or "collective memory." One can therefore think of the Bible as including, or indeed embodying, the corporate memory of Israel and of the Second Temple community and of the early Christian community. It comprises what they wanted to remember or wanted people to remember or wanted to be remembered by. Remembering is the task of the people of God, and its resource.

Narrative is then a regular way in which an individual or a group organizes its memory, and the Scriptures are dominated by narratives that articulate a memory of the past in the form that these cultures wanted to affirm. Admittedly, the word *narrative*, along with the word *metanarrative* and the idea of a "grand narrative," are cultural clichés from mid- and late-twentieth-century philosophy and theology. To restore their usefulness, it is helpful to go behind the clichés. The key figure who is referenced in much of the study of metanarrative is Jean-François Lyotard, and in this context talk about narrative and about a grand narrative sometimes simply has in mind ideas or theories or worldviews.[2] In the use of the word *metanarrative*, the emphasis has thus come to lie on *meta* rather than *narrative*; the word suggests a master idea or a set of master ideas, some form of transcendent and universal truth, but not necessarily an overarching story.

The Scriptures, however, begin as an actual narrative about the Beginning, and from time to time they speak narratively or quasi-narratively about the End, while in the meantime they focus on the events that take the world from Beginning to End. As with any story, when one comes to the end it is possible and perhaps natural to reflect on its implications as a whole, and on the chief characters we have met. One could say that it is the function of biblical theology to do so.

Middle Narratives

In a more traditional sense, then, a narrative is an account of a sequence of events. The link between narrative and worldview is that narrative is a natural carrier of a worldview. Narratives that fulfill this function are prom-

---

[2]See, famously, Jean-François Lyotard, *The Postmodern Condition* (Minneapolis: University of Minnesota, 1984), pp. xxiv-xxv; and, e.g., David K. Naugle's articulating of the question, "Is there a metanarrative, an ultimate *Weltanschauung* that explains all other worldviews?" (*Worldview: The History of a Concept* [Grand Rapids: Eerdmans, 2002], p. 320).

inent in the Bible, and it is narrative in this sense that we will consider in this chapter. In the Bible and in Christian thinking, vital importance attaches to a grand narrative that is indeed narrative in form, a total worldview expressed in a story that embraces Beginning and End and the crucial events on the narrative line in between.

What I call "middle narratives" articulate a memory of the past on a smaller scale, as the form of or as part of the memory that a particular culture wanted to affirm. I base the notion of middle narratives on the idea of middle axioms in ethics. One significance that can attach to the idea of middle axioms is that they articulate tenets lying between concrete imperatives and general principles. The Bible talks both in terms of specific duties such as "build a wall around the roof of your house" and of general obligations such as "love your neighbor." Middle axioms help mediate between these by providing tenets that are less specific than the former but more concrete than the latter: for example, "Ensure that your house is a safe place for people."

In parallel, the two Testaments contain many short narratives expressing theological insights: stories about Israel, about individual Israelites, about Jesus and about the infant church. They also imply a grand theological narrative, which the creeds aim to encapsulate. But in addition, the two Testaments include a series of extensive explicit or implicit middle narratives, which form a key way in which the Scriptures do theology.

In this chapter I examine the theological implications of some of these middle narratives, consider how they may be seen as part of a grand theological narrative that emerges from the two Testaments as a whole and is a key aspect of biblical theology, and consider the relationship between the middle narratives and the grand narrative. I note that one needs to understand the middle narratives in order to be able to articulate the grand narrative and that one needs to understand the grand narrative in order to understand the broader significance of the middle narratives.

In practice, Christians commonly work with assumptions about the Christian grand narrative that leave out the thrust of the First Testament middle narratives and, indeed, do poor justice to the thrust of the New Testament middle narratives. Further, we unconsciously incorporate in that grand narrative lines from a different narrative, one deriving from our own culture. Our understanding of the biblical grand narrative is then inevitably skewed.

Further, the First Testament middle narratives have unrealized potential for helping the church live its life in the context of that biblical grand narrative. This fact opens up a further aspect of the question whether we need the New Testament, or whether we lose out by thinking that all we need is the New Testament, or (more subtly) by assuming that our construct of the grand narrative does justice to either Testament.

The Bible is not a love letter to us from God; it does not focus on a personal relationship between God and the individual. Nor does it focus on a challenge to work for peace and justice or on adherence to a body of doctrinal beliefs. Nor does it focus on faith itself: "The Gospel is not primarily concerned with faith" but with "that upon which the faith reposes," with the object of faith, "the *kerygma* that arouses faith."[3] It suggests a grand narrative about a project that God initiated and will bring to completion. Human communities and individuals gain their significance through being drawn into that project. We see ourselves in light of its beginning at creation and its consummation at Jesus' appearing. Israel sees itself in light of what God did at the exodus and at Sinai. After Jesus' coming, the community sees itself in light of his death and resurrection. Israel looks forward to the time when God will put all things right. The church is a body that "waits for the revealing of our Lord Jesus Christ, who will also keep us firm until the end, unaccused, on the day of our Lord Jesus" (1 Cor 1:7-8).

The narrative focus of the Bible makes "witness" an illuminating image to describe it, though "witness" is another cliché from mid- and late-twentieth-century theology that it is necessary to get behind. A witness is someone who is in a position to testify to an event. We do stretch the term in using the expression *character witness*, someone who can speak of a person's character on the basis of acquaintance with his or her life. The Bible, then, is "testimony pointing beyond itself to a divine reality to which it bears witness."[4] But the notion of witness needs to keep its connotation of testimony to events.

The Bible does not give its witness in the form of one continuous story. Its most extended witness takes the form of what I call middle narratives.

---

[3]J. K. S. Reid, *Our Life in Christ* (London: SCM, 1963), p. 7.
[4]Brevard S. Childs, *Biblical Theology of the Old and New Testament* (Minneapolis: Fortress, 1993), p. 9.

Genesis–Kings

[handwritten annotation: Creation to collapse (exile). the thwarting of God's plan by the ppl, yet possible hope...]

Its first middle narrative is Genesis–Kings, a *grand* theological narrative in its own right. At one level it is one long exercise in memory and in memory formation. I take it as reaching its final form not long after the last event it relates, during the exile; it embodies a way of understanding Israel's history from its beginnings to the time of the community for which it was written. This assumption about its date goes against a trend in First Testament study to read it as reflecting the Persian period, but I don't think my reading will be greatly affected if one takes that approach. Conversely, I also assume that much of the contents have a long history, and I am not averse to the idea that it had seen earlier editions, but I am focusing on the work as we have it.

One way to read it involves focusing on the significance of four key figures: Abraham, Moses, Joshua and David. Abraham stands for the way Israel's life is lived in the context of God's promise to Israel's ancestors. Moses stands for the assertion that Yahweh reigns as king in the world and over Israel, not least by means of his instructions for its life. Joshua stands for the people's entering into possession of Canaan. David stands for the way Israel's life is lived in the Promised Land in the context of God's commitment to him and to Jerusalem. But the story in which these four figures stand out is framed by two further motifs characterized by some ambiguity. The story begins with God's creation of the world and of humanity as a whole, so that Genesis sees God's involvement with Israel as designed to fulfill God's intention to bless the world, yet that motif all but disappears within the main story. The main story eventually ends with the unraveling of all that has preceded, as the people find themselves back in the Babylonia from which Abraham had been summoned, a fate that overwhelms them because more often than not they flout the will of their sovereign, which had been expressed through Moses. It results in their losing the land into whose possession Joshua led them. The Davidic monarchy comes to an end. The First Testament has been called the story of the miscarriage of God's plan.[5] This understanding is inappropriate as a summary of the First Testament as a whole, but it is a fair description of Genesis–Kings.

Reading the story in Genesis–Kings during the exile, in whatever form it

---

[5]See Rudolf Bultmann, "Prophecy and Fulfillment," in *Essays on Old Testament Interpretation*, ed. C. Westermann (London: SCM, 1963) = *Essays on Old Testament Hermeneutics* (Richmond: Knox, 1963), pp. 50-75.

had, would thus be a sobering experience for Judahites. Indeed, how could it not be wholly discouraging? There are several sorts of answers to that question. One might start from the description of the Books of Kings, in particular, as a *Gerichtsdoxologie*, an act of praise at the justice of God's judgment.[6] Admittedly, memory studies suggest that this description is not quite right, because a *Gerichtsdoxologie* would need to be addressed to God; the Books of Kings are addressed to people, as a statement of how they need to remember their past. But some of the implications of that description are unaffected: the books invite people to face the facts about their story, and in this sense to make their own *Gerichtsdoxologie*. It will involve their standing naked and vulnerable before God (or owning that such is their position). Given their story, all they can do is cast themselves on God's mercy. But one encouragement toward their doing so is the way God has shown himself characterized by faithfulness and mercy through their story. Perhaps these qualities have not come to an end, as Lamentations declares (e.g., Lam 3:22-32). Another form of encouragement in the story is God's making his promises to Abraham, as 2 Kings 13:23 notes. More prominent is God's making his promises to David, which have inhibited God from casting off David's successors (1 Kings 15:4; 2 Kings 8:19; 19:34; 20:6). The closing scene of 2 Kings, relating the release of King Jehoiakin in exile, constitutes a sign that God has not abandoned these promises. The note in 2 Kings 6:1 that dates the temple building in the 480th year after the Israelites left Egypt likewise hints at a scheme that divides Israel's history into periods of twelve generations, one from Abraham to Moses, one from Moses to Solomon, one from Solomon to the fall of Jerusalem—and one beginning with the temple restoration (the note adds support to the idea that the narrative in its final form belongs in the Second Temple period).

A more challenging answer to the question how the story in Genesis–Kings would read in the context of the exile would be its copious reference to the teaching of Moses. The Judahites cannot expect to find mercy or the fulfillment of Yahweh's promises unless they are now prepared to make a more serious commitment to this teaching.[7]

---

[6]Gerhard von Rad, *Old Testament Theology* (Edinburgh: Oliver and Boyd, 1962), 1:357-58; cf. "Gerichtsdoxologie," *Gesammelte Studien zum Alten Testament* (Munich: Kaiser, 1973), 2:245-54.
[7]I owe this point to a comment made by Zvi Shimon when I gave an earlier version of this chapter at a Society of Biblical Literature meeting in July 2013.

The plot line of this first middle narrative, then, follows the sequence creation, disaster, promise, serfdom, deliverance, revelation, land, order, collapse. It declares that God has a purpose for the world as a whole, that his plans for implementing his purpose have not so far been fulfilled, that likewise he has not been able to fulfill his purpose for Israel to be the means of implementing that purpose, but that all might not be lost.

CHRONICLES–EZRA–NEHEMIAH; DANIEL

The Scriptures' second middle narrative is Chronicles–Ezra–Nehemiah. Again, I do not assume that this narrative came into existence in one go, but the overlap between the closing verses of Chronicles and the opening of Ezra invites readers to read these works sequentially, even if Ezra–Nehemiah was written first, and even though the most familiar order within the Torah, the Prophets and the Writings puts Ezra–Nehemiah ahead of Chronicles. It is also clear that these verses situate Chronicles–Ezra–Nehemiah in a time at least a few decades after the little note of hope at the end of 2 Kings, which refers to the release of King Jehoiakin in 561. Chronicles knows that Cyrus's conquest of Babylon in 539 was a more significant indication that Yahweh was still at work. The reference to Cyrus leads into the account of the restoration of the temple in Ezra; the policies of subsequent Persian kings make possible the further works of restoration by Ezra and Nehemiah.

Chronicles begins its actual recounting of Israel's story with David; the story from Adam through Abraham, Moses and Joshua to Saul is told by means of a list of names occupying the first third of 1 Chronicles. Its account of David's importance then focuses on his significance for the temple, which links with the importance of the temple in the account of the return from exile in Ezra 1–6. One could thus say that the three key figures in *this* middle narrative are David, Ezra and Nehemiah, and that its focus lies on Jerusalem: its temple and its worship, Ezra's renewal of its life, and Nehemiah's rebuilding of its walls.

There is again some ambiguity about this middle narrative. Beginning with Adam, the first human being, throws into sharper light its subsequent omission of any reference to God's purpose for humanity as a whole. On the other hand, its treatment of emperors such as Cyrus, Darius and Artaxerxes gives them a more positive relationship to Israel and to Yahweh's purpose than one finds in references to emperors in Genesis–Kings. At the same time, Chronicles–Ezra–Nehemiah frets over the fact that the community is still under the control of a superpower. While it sees Yahweh as having fulfilled his promise to restore Israel after the exile, it portrays the Second Temple community as struggling in various ways with adversity and with its own failure. And it does not reach any closure. At the end of Nehemiah, the story simply stops. God's purpose for Israel is thus semi-fulfilled.

The third middle narrative I consider is the one expressed in the visions in Daniel. Here the superpowers, which were more prominent in Chronicles–Ezra–Nehemiah than in Genesis–Kings, come into the forefront of the narrative; and in association with that fact, the visions declare that God is going to bring his purpose for the world to its consummation. The sequence of superpowers comprises Babylon, Medo-Persia and Greece. Daniel may be picking up an older scheme that began with Assyria, the actual first Middle Eastern superpower; if so, the scheme has been adapted to fit a framework that begins with the time of Daniel himself, living in the Babylonian period. At the other end, the scheme later gets adapted to include Rome, and eventually to cover subsequent superpowers. But within Daniel, the scheme embraces Babylon, Medo-Persia and Greece, which in due course give way to the implementing of God's reign through his people. This middle narrative, then, offers a perspective on the entire history of Israel from the exile to the End.

In Daniel 7 the animals that symbolize the empires emerge from the sea. It is likely a negative image, a symbol of dynamic power that at best operates independently of God, at worst constitutes an embodiment of mayhem and havoc; in the new heavens and the new earth in Revelation 21, there is no more sea. The vision does not go back to creation (if it did so, it would offer a complete grand narrative) but begins with the emergence of the superpowers. Their sequence involves neither consistent degeneration nor progress. Babylon is bad, Medo-Persia is less awful, Greece is truly bad. The evaluation corresponds to Judah's experience at the hand of the empires. The last of the visions is noteworthy for its detailed account of the conflicts between the Seleucid and Ptolemaic monarchies and their relationship with Judah, which stands between them. The theological significance of this account is the way it portrays history as going nowhere, a tale "full of sound and fury, signifying nothing." Yes,

> To-morrow, and to-morrow, and to-morrow,
> Creeps in this petty pace from day to day
> To the last syllable of recorded time.[8]

Yet the visions do not portray history as petering out or just jogging along, as might be the implication of our first two narratives. When it has reached its darkest point, and when the last superpower in the sequence has reached a height of arrogance and blasphemy in relation to God and of oppression of God's people, God intervenes, terminates the superpower's rule and gives over power to his saints. The visions were vindicated by the defeat and withdrawal of the Seleucid forces from Jerusalem in 164, after which Judah gained control of its own destiny, though it held it only for a century until the next superpower arrived.

The narrative expounded by Daniel's visions also complements the one in Genesis–Kings, which offers a perspective on the story from creation to the exile. Indeed, combining these two generates a First Testament grand narrative. Its first half takes the story from the world's creation to a plan that reaches miscarriage under the Babylonians. Its second half exponentially increases that gloom as it sets Israel's continuing story against the backcloth of the history of the world as a whole from the Babylonian empire onward, a history that has no meaning, but it declares that the absence of meaning from history does not indicate that miscarriage has the last word or that things are out of God's control. The goal of history will not be reached by Israel's obedience or by the nations' initiative, but it will be reached by God's intervention. God's purpose for Israel and for the nations will reach fulfillment.

ISAIAH, JEREMIAH, EZEKIEL

Neither the three middle narratives we have considered nor the First Testament grand narrative that emerges from combining them incorporates a messianic figure. One factor behind this lack is that the overt focus of works that take narrative form lies on the past. There are other middle narratives one could infer from the First Testament, notably from Isaiah, from Jeremiah and from Ezekiel, that do incorporate such a figure; a prophet's implicit

---

[8]Those words were uttered by Macbeth in Dunsinane Castle, twenty miles from St. Andrews, Scotland, the location of the meeting mentioned in the previous note.

middle narrative by its nature makes more overt reference to the future. The antithesis "earlier things" and "new things" (Is 42:9) suggests more broadly a way of summarizing the prophetic middle narratives. The books of Isaiah, Jeremiah and Ezekiel take Israel from faithlessness to the New Jerusalem.

In Isaiah, the reference of "earlier things" may vary, and it can be difficult to be sure whether it alludes to creation or the promise to Israel's ancestors or the exodus or the downfall of Judah or the beginning of Cyrus's campaign to take control of the Babylonian empire. The book of Isaiah makes a few overt references to creation, the ancestors and the exodus (e.g., Is 42:5; 43:4; 51:2; 63:7-14) but it focuses on the period of the empires' importance in Judah's life, the period of pressure from, and the downfall of, Assyria, Babylon and Persia. Its middle narrative thus focuses on Judah and Jerusalem, as its opening verse announces. Judah's story is one of failing to trust in Yahweh and of giving in to fear and the instinct to try to ensure one's security (not least by seeking help from Egypt) in light of the difficulty of believing that Yahweh will do so. It is the story of Yahweh's acting on Judah's blindness, not least by deepening it, and of Yahweh's proving himself in promising and bringing about Assyria's fall, though also of his envisaging a time when Assyria (and Egypt) will worship with Judah. It is then the story of Judah's similar false trust in Babylon, its continuing blindness, and its inclination to continue being overimpressed by Babylon's gods and their images. It is also the story of Yahweh's proving himself in promising and bringing about Babylon's fall, which will in addition make possible the recognition of Yahweh by the imperial power and by other nations. It is the story of Judah's expression of that lack of trust in Yahweh that takes the form of turning to other so-called deities, yet also of Yahweh's continuing intention to bring about the glorious restoration of Jerusalem as the veritable embodiment of a new heavens and a new earth, and of Yahweh's drawing the nations to acknowledge him.

Jeremiah's middle narrative starts further back than Isaiah's in the sense that it has more interest in telling the story that starts with the exodus and the wilderness period. Yahweh looked after his bride during that time and initially she kept her commitment to him, but in the land she became unfaithful and turned to other deities. Yahweh has therefore chastised her. The situation is going to get horrendously worse, but repudiation will not be the end. Yahweh will restore Ephraim and Judah and write his teaching into their minds instead of merely setting it before their eyes. The kings who do not live up to the Davidic ideal will be succeeded by a king who will live up to it.

Jeremiah has a prominent place in an influential modern articulation of the biblical grand narrative. According to this understanding, Jeremiah's letter encouraging Judahites to settle down in Babylon (Jer 29) designates the exile as not a two-generation parenthesis in Israel's life after which normal political life under a Davidic king in Canaan would resume, but as the beginning of a new nonpolitical existence.[9] This understanding does not survive a study of Jeremiah 29 or other passages in the book. When the prophet urges Judahites to settle down in Babylon, he does so on the basis of the fact that there will be no speedy return to Judah; but when people turn to Yahweh, Yahweh will gather them and other scattered Judahites and bring them back to Judah (Jer 29:14; cf., e.g., Jer 30:3; 31:3-25). It is not Jeremiah but Isaiah 40–66 that totally relativizes kingship in Judah by making Cyrus the only king and turning Israel back into the kingly people that it was at Sinai (Ex 19:6; Is 55:3-5). Isaiah 40–66 draws the radical conclusion that Jeremiah does not draw, though Isaiah 40–66 also has the exiles returning to Judah, not settling forever in dispersion.

Ezekiel is more radical than Jeremiah in a different direction. His middle narrative starts from Egypt, the exodus and the wilderness, but his portrait of Israel's relationship with Yahweh sees Israel as unfaithful from the beginning. His bigger surprise is that his narrative future does not end with the restoration of a covenant relationship that will be "forever," living in the land "forever," ruled by David "forever," with Yahweh's sanctuary among them "forever" (Ezek 37:24-28). After Israel is once again living in safety in its land, Israel will be subject to a further invasion from the north, but it will also see a great act of judgment on its attackers (Ezek 38:1–39:29); there follows a much fuller vision of the restoration of the land and the temple (Ezek 40:1–48:35). Ezekiel thus makes more explicit a fact that implicitly arises from the work of the other prophets. What they describe as the End never is the End. One could argue that Ezekiel is a more important landmark within the First Testament than Jeremiah, because he articulates the pattern that will also be instanced by the beginnings of Christian faith (as we noted

---

[9]John H. Yoder, *For the Nations* (Grand Rapids: Eerdmans, 1997), pp. 51-65.

in chapter three). You would have thought that Jesus was bringing the End; but it turns out that history continues.

MARK, MATTHEW, LUKE–ACTS, JOHN

While the New Testament middle narratives belong to the other side of the chronological gap between the Testaments, they are about as near temporally to Daniel's visions as Daniel's visions are to Chronicles–Ezra–Nehemiah (two hundred years or so in both cases), and temporally they are much nearer to Daniel's visions than Daniel's visions are to Genesis–Kings.[10]

Mark's Gospel has so short a time frame, three years, that arguably it hardly counts as a middle narrative. Most of the Gospel relates incidents from Jesus' ministry; the last third covers the closing week of his life; one final paragraph relates his resurrection. Whether this brief ending is original or something has been lost, readers apparently thought its brevity unsatisfactory, and added alternative endings to take the narrative on into the story of the proclaiming of the gospel. Within Mark's own work, for our purposes more significance attaches to Jesus' declarations in Mark 13 about a coming persecution, a desolating sacrilege and an appearing of the "Man." If we take Mark 13 into account, this middle narrative extends forward in a parallel way to Daniel's visions, from which it derives its imagery. Yet its focus lies resolutely on Jesus' story, and its implication for its readers is that they need to focus resolutely on the life and death of Jesus, and on the coming crisis and its resolution to which Mark 13 refers. While it emphasizes that Jesus is the fulfillment of First Testament prophecy, especially Isaiah, it does not emphasize Jesus' relationship to the First Testament story.[11]

Matthew's middle narrative also takes Jesus' story forward with a brief account of events following the resurrection, and it incorporates Jesus' declarations concerning what Matthew calls his coming and the end of the age. It includes the prospect that the story's plot will continue in making disciples of the nations. It contrasts with Mark in a more striking fashion in the way it takes Jesus' story back from his ministry to his birth, and behind his birth to his ancestry; the account traces Jesus' origins into the past, to Abraham

---

[10]That is, I date Genesis–Kings in the sixth century; Chronicles–Ezra–Nehemiah about 400–350 B.C.; Daniel in the 160s B.C.; Mark about A.D. 60; Matthew, Luke–Acts, and John later in the first century.

[11]Against Rikki E. Watts, *Isaiah's New Exodus in Mark* (reprinted Grand Rapids: Baker, 2000).

via the exile and David. While Mark referred to the beginning of Jesus' ministry as a fulfillment of First Testament prophecy and utilized First Testament imagery to portray the coming crisis, he did not attach any significance to the First Testament story itself. In contrast, Matthew portrays Jesus as the logical culmination of Israel's story. His structuring it in that threefold way (Abraham, David, the exile) interestingly ignores the exodus, like Chronicles. But Matthew thus from the beginning makes a link with Israel's story and invites its readers to see themselves as living in light of a more substantial middle narrative than Mark's.

Luke's story extends the narrative further. First, it tells even more about the background to Jesus' birth, and does so in a way that implicitly links Jesus' story onto Chronicles–Ezra–Nehemiah. The community into which Jesus is born is the community that David, Ezra and Nehemiah established. As we have them, the familiar order of the Torah, the Prophets and the Writings that closes with Chronicles is a Jewish order, whereas the order ending with the Prophets, and in particular with Malachi, is the order in Christian Bibles. In origin, quite likely both are Jewish orders, and in content the Hebrew order leads just as suggestively into the New Testament (furthermore, the last word in the Christian order, in Malachi, is the word *ḥērem*, annihilation, which one might not think too welcome a lead-in to the gospel story). Luke incorporates a different account of Jesus' ancestry from Matthew's, an account that traces this ancestry back to Adam. Luke's narrative thus again recalls Chronicles. But Luke's much more striking extension of his middle narrative comes when his Gospel leads into a second book, almost as long as the first, relating how the Jesus story spread through Jesus' home country and then around the Eastern Mediterranean to Rome. Luke–Acts parallels Chronicles–Ezra–Nehemiah further in the way it comes to a stop rather than to a conclusion. Readers know that more must have followed the last events that are related in Acts, but they do not discover the nature of the continuing story.

John's version of the story traces Jesus back to the beginning in an even more decisive fashion. Mark is content to relate the beginning of the gospel, and even Genesis is satisfied with looking back to the beginning of creation. But Proverbs 8:22-31 goes behind creation to what had been the case before the world existed, in order to point out that God already had Wisdom, and John 1 follows the example of Proverbs. It declares that this Wisdom, the Mind or Message,[12] was there in the beginning, before the world's creation. John's Gospel is then the account of the Mind/Message in the beginning, as the One through whom God created the world, as made flesh and as returning to God. The Father's sending Jesus is a key motif in John.[13] There are a number of ways of describing Jesus' coming. It is like someone in power sending a representative on a mission. It is like someone from a higher domain (from the upper city) visiting the lower domain (the lower city). It is like someone who belongs to the spiritual realm changing into someone who also belongs to the material realm. In each case the move is a temporary one; eventually the person returns. This narrative arc is key for John. In between the beginning and the end of the story, John puts christological statements on Jesus' lips in a way that is historically anachronistic. Jesus did not say things such as "the Father and I are one" or "before Abraham was, I am" or "I am the resurrection and the life." But putting such sayings onto his lips during his ministry and integrally relating them to his deeds anchors them to his ministry and affirms that the human Jesus really was God's son incarnate.[14] Yes, "the message was *theos*." The Gospel as a whole makes clear that John does not mean either that Jesus is a second deity or that he fully comprises God.[15] The Message was divine. Like the signs in Exodus, the signs in John should logically generate recognition, submission and trust, but there is no compulsion for them to do so. The signs foreshadow the major event that is coming.

ROMANS

As is the case in the First Testament, there are further middle narratives that we can infer from the New Testament's non-narrative works. One could say that Revelation's middle narrative is a mirror image of the one in the Gospels as it takes people from suffering to the New Jerusalem. Not surprisingly,

---

[12]John's use of *logos* resonates with that in Philo, where *logos* means something like "mind," but later in John and elsewhere in the New Testament it means "teaching" or "message" (not least in expressions such as "the *logos* of God" or "the *logos* of Christ" [e.g., Col 1:25; 3:16]), and both "mind" and "teaching/message" make sense in Jn 1.

[13]Cf. Martin Hengel, "The Prologue of the Gospel of John as the Gateway to Christological Truth," in *The Gospel of John and Christian Theology*, ed. Richard Bauckham and Carl Mosser (Grand Rapids: Eerdmans, 2008), pp. 265-94 (p. 268).

[14]Cf. D. Moody Smith, *The Theology of the Gospel of John* (Cambridge: Cambridge University Press, 1995), p. 110.

[15]Cf. Larry W. Hurtado, *Lord Jesus Christ: Devotion to Jesus in Earliest Christianity* (Grand Rapids: Eerdmans, 2003), p. 369.

Romans, as Paul's most systematic letter, gives us a most comprehensive account of his middle narrative, which covers creation, disobedience, wrath, promise, revelation, disobedience, fulfillment, disobedience, proclamation and consummation, in a profound revisionist account of the story that appears in the First Testament and in the Gospels. When Paul says that Jesus died and was raised "in accordance with the Scriptures," he is not referring to the fulfillment of isolated texts but "to the entire biblical narrative as the story which has reached its climax in the Messiah." Although he could note specific texts in the Psalms and Isaiah 40–55, "Paul is primarily concerned with the entire sweep of biblical narrative."[16]

His implicit middle narrative (one could argue that it is indeed an implicit grand narrative) begins with God's creation of the world and God's creation of humanity, then goes on to humanity's disobedience to God with its devastating effect on the rest of humanity, and to an account of God's wrath then working out in the world. He here follows Genesis and subsequent Scriptures, but he draws out further theological implications from them. He continues to do so in his account of Abraham, making explicit and stressing a point implicit in Genesis that God related to Abraham and made promises to him on the basis of his grace, to which Abraham needed simply to respond in trust; outward observances came only later. Without any reference to the exodus, Paul then leaps on to the revelation at Sinai and makes a bolder comment on its significance. The First Testament itself makes clear that Israel was not very good at living by the Sinai revelation; this revelation simply turned Israel more clearly into sinners. Like the retelling of Genesis–Kings in Chronicles, Paul's retelling of the First Testament story in Romans and Galatians emerges from his own context, from his looking back in light of Jesus' coming[17] and from his needing to deal with the mistaken understanding of the place of the law that appears among the Galatians and elsewhere. His interpreting of the place of the law is in fact similar to his subsequent related interpreting of the story of Sarah and Hagar (Gal 4:21-31). Paul is not making a theoretical point about salvation history but a point that arises from the situation in his own day.

So the law (Paul points out) was neither the basis of Israel's relationship with God nor the basis of its living in that relationship. God brought about

---

[16]N. T. Wright, *The Resurrection of the Son of God* (London: SPCK, 2003), pp. 320-21.

[17]Cf. E. P. Sanders, *Paul, the Law, and the Jewish People* (Philadelphia: Fortress, 1983), pp. 65-91.

the deliverance of both Jews and Gentiles through Jesus' dying for them, and they now live in obedience to God. The Galatians behave as if doing things the Torah says could give life, as Leviticus 18:5 implies: "The person who does these things will live by them" (Gal 3:12). Paul denies that it can do so, and speaks more negatively about that statement in the Torah than he does in Romans 10:5. He hardly intends to contradict the Torah itself; more likely his concern is with the significance the Galatians are attaching to it.[18]

The puzzle is that the Jewish people have been no more responsive to the message about Jesus than they have been to the message from Sinai. How could it be? Why has God not opened their eyes to see God's splendor in Jesus' face, as God did for Paul himself on the way to Damascus? In this connection, too, Paul searches through the First Testament narrative in order to be able to develop a narrative of his own that makes sense of the question. His answer is that the law indeed only made Israel's own situation worse, but that Israel's rebellion could facilitate God's revelation to the nations. It is through the Jewish people's rejection of Jesus that the spread of the gospel comes to focus on the Gentiles, though God will then use this flourishing among the Gentiles as a means of attracting the Jews. This revisionist understanding is indeed a *mystērion*: not a "mystery" in the sense of something strange and unintelligible but in the sense the word has when referring to a mystery novel, a story that comes to a denouement such as one could hardly have guessed yet such as explains what has come before. The mystery comes to be revealed by means of the prophetic writings, but only when someone such as Paul pores over them in light of the actual event of Jewish rejection and Gentile response and sees clues they now provide (Rom 16:25-26). God's intention was always that the whole world should join in worship, praise and hope, and God always made that intention clear; Romans 15:8-16 proves the point by means of a series of scriptural quotations that require no Christian reinterpretation in order to make them assert Paul's point.

Paul came to his understanding of the story by starting from its denouement and working backwards. He knew that God had acted in Jesus to bring about the salvation of the whole world, Gentile as well as Jew, and it

---

[18]See further the discussion of Torah in chapter three above.

was from that fact that he worked out why such action was necessary. "In his preaching he did not *start* from man's need, but from God's deed." This explains his somewhat convoluted understanding of the place of the law in the scheme of things; "it is the Gentile question and the exclusivism of Paul's soteriology which dethrone the law, not a misunderstanding of it or a view predetermined by his background."[19]

EPHESIANS

Ephesians talks further about the *mystērion* of God's will. What God has been doing in history as a whole is a secret that is now revealed. Three times in its initial exposition of the gospel Ephesians talks about God's will; it also refers to God's choice or election, God's predestining or foreordaining, God's pleasure or desire, God's purpose, and God's intention. "God chose us in Christ before the world's foundation to be holy and faultless before him in love,[20] having predestined us for adoption as sons in relation to him though Jesus Christ, in accordance with the pleasure of his will, to the praise of his majestic grace." He made this grace abound toward us "in all wisdom and insight, having made known to us the secret of his will in accordance with his pleasure, which he set forth in Christ for implementation when the time had fully come, to gather into one all things through Christ, things in the heavens and on the earth." Thus "in Christ we have also been allocated [to God], having been predestined in accordance with the intention of the one who makes all things work according to the purpose he willed, so that we might be for the praise of his majesty" (Eph 1:4-12). The object of the choice of this people is God's own honor; the focus compares with that in Ezekiel.

The identity of the "we" in this exposition changes; at the end it denotes Jews who have come to trust in Jesus (the succeeding sentence refers to Gentile believers), but at the beginning it probably denotes the Jewish-Gentile church, and further in the background of the exposition is God's earlier selection of Israel. In any of the connections, the translation "select" for *eklegomai* could be misleading insofar as it implies excluding others. But to describe Jesus as God's "chosen one" (Lk 9:35;

---

[19]E. P. Sanders, *Paul and Palestinian Judaism* (Philadelphia: Fortress, 1977), pp. 444, 497.
[20]"In love" might go with what precedes or what follows: see NRSV over against TNIV.

23:35) is not to imply that God chose Jesus and excluded others.[21] Further, the goal of this choosing does not directly or explicitly relate to these groups' eternal destiny but to God's present purpose. They are chosen in order that God's grace may be recognized, in order to bring unity to all God's creation, and in order that God's purpose may be fulfilled. Like most processes of choice, they serve the purpose of the one who chose them, and do so in the present not in eternity.

The opening statement in the letter makes little reference to sin or to Jesus' death. One could infer that God's working via this choice was not a response to human sin but was part of God's original intention.[22] This possibility fits with its having been part of God's intention before creation. Was it then always God's plan to work via Israel? Or was humanity the intended object of God's election, the means of bringing about unity in everything and of promoting God's praise? "This is the secret that is finally revealed to the saints: God loved them before the creation."[23]

Also consistent among these alternatives is the reference to a body; God's election does not have in mind individuals. Elsewhere the Scriptures indeed speak of God's selection of individuals such as Abraham, David and Paul, but again this election relates to God's purpose for the world, God's desire to bless the world and God's recognition by the world. One cannot universalize from God's selection of such individuals to God's selection of each individual within Israel or the church. When the Scriptures describe the way other individuals such as Jethro, Rahab, the Ethiopian politician or Cornelius come to belong to Israel or the church, they sometimes see this process as issuing from God's revelation to these people as individuals and sometimes as issuing from their insight and trust in response to evidence that is in principle available to anyone. If one were to tell a dozen people about Jesus and six were to respond by recognizing him while six did not, one could say that the response of the six issued from God's purpose that there should be a body to achieve God's purpose and proclaim God's grace, but it is not clear that the Scriptures imply that the first six responded be-

---

[21]Cf. T. K. Abbott, *A Critical and Exegetical Commentary on the Epistles to the Ephesians and to the Colossians* (New York: Scribner, 1897), p. 6.

[22]Cf. Markus Barth, *Ephesians* (Garden City, NY: Doubleday, 1974), 1:104.

[23]Ibid., 1:127.

cause they were individually chosen or that the six who did not respond did so because they were not selected. The Scriptures do not push the imagery to this logical conclusion, and one has to be wary of pushing imagery to its logical conclusion. Ephesians may thus sidestep the concern about the relationship between divine sovereignty and human freewill that has sometimes concerned Christians. Having a body that will fulfill the purposes described in Ephesians 1 is God's sovereign intent. Who constitutes that body is utterly negotiable. If there are not six respondents from this proclamation, God will inspire another proclamation or dangle the truth more attractively or more forcefully in front of people, though the decision whether or not to recognize it will still be theirs. If there actually are six respondents, one might still bear in mind the prayer attributed in the United Kingdom to C. H. Spurgeon and in the United States to D. L. Moody: "Lord, save all the elect, and then elect some more."

The move between speaking of Israel, of Jewish believers, of Gentile believers and of the Jewish-Gentile body itself makes this point as it nuances or qualifies the declarations about God's sovereign will, even while making these declarations. God's design is to be achieved through Israel, through a group within Israel, through a largely Gentile body. According to Romans 9–11, that intention of God's goes back to the beginning. Did God directly design the entirety of human history to work out the way it has? It seems counterintuitive to see all history with its wickedness and with the Jewish people's refusal to recognize the Messiah as God's ideal will, and unwise to speak in terms of a "plan" God had that has resulted in things turning out as they have.[24] More likely they are consequences of God's will that humanity should be responsible for its own decisions. The implementing of God's overall purpose then interacted with humanity's exercise of that responsibility. God determined to work via human decision making and to be flexible about how the purpose should be fulfilled. It is for this reason that (as we noted in chapter two) humanity can hasten the coming of God's day (2 Pet 3:12)—or delay it. Such insight into the nature of God's activity in history and thus into the life of God's people runs through the whole of the Scriptures.

---

[24]Cf. Barth's comments, ibid., 1:65, 87.

THE GRAND NARRATIVE AND THE MIDDLE NARRATIVES

Different parts of the Scriptures thus hint at a grand narrative or suggest that there is one, but they no more expound a grand narrative than they expound a theology. They present us with a series of explicit or implicit narratives, on smaller and larger scales. The Bible is not directly a grand narrative, but both Testaments incorporate a number of grandish narratives, extensive expositions of part of God's story. In focusing on the Scriptures' middle narratives, then, I am not giving up the idea of a grand narrative, though I have questions about the common forms of the Christian grand narrative that leap straight from creation to Jesus, as Christian creeds do, or that comprise only creation, fall, redemption in Christ and the second coming. These involve gross oversimplification.

What I call middle narratives are not so different from what Lyotard calls "little narratives" or "local narratives," which he does regard as the nearest we can get to a "grand narrative."[25] Paul Ricoeur has likewise commented that "the birth of the concept of history as a collective singular, under which the collection of particular histories is placed, marks the bridging of the greatest gap imaginable between unitary history and the unlimited multiplicity of individual memories and the plurality of collective memories." The trouble is, Ricoeur comments, that human plurality "chips away from within the very concept of history as a collective singular"; special histories resist globalization.[26] In examining the Jewish understanding of memory, Yosef Yerushalmi has noted that the Greeks did not find ultimate meaning in history as a whole.[27] Perhaps they were wise. Ricoeur's observation coheres with Ecclesiastes's way of looking at things, in particular the lament that God has put "eternity" (hā'ōlām) in humanity's mind, yet has not enabled people to fathom it (Eccles 3:11). There is thus no total history in the First Testament itself, even in Daniel, though we have seen that there are some pretty grand narratives and that the adding of Daniel to Genesis–Kings and Chronicles–Ezra–Nehemiah within the First Testament makes it not a huge leap to infer a grand narrative from the First Testament. Likewise the narratives we might

---

[25]See, e.g., Jean-François Lyotard, "Universal History and Cultural Differences," in *The Lyotard Reader* (Oxford: Blackwell, 1989), pp. 314-23.

[26]Paul Ricoeur, *Memory, History, Forgetting* (Chicago: University of Chicago, 2004), pp. 299, 301.

[27]Yosef Hayim Yerushalmi, *Zakhor: Jewish History and Jewish Memory* (reprinted New York: Schocken, 1989), p. 7.

infer from John and Paul (and from Revelation) look pretty grand. In seeking to articulate a grand narrative on the basis of the Scriptures, then, we are undertaking a task of which the individual biblical writers may not have dreamt, though no more so than in other aspects of biblical theology, and we are undertaking a task that is not alien to the Scriptures overall.

Taken as a whole, the New Testament middle narratives embrace the First Testament grand narrative and nuance it in light of Jesus. Or perhaps the point should be put the other way around: they set their own middle narratives in the context of the First Testament grand narrative. They have nothing much to add to the First Testament's account of the past up until the story of the last empire. What they do (in common with other Jewish understandings of the day) is extend and nuance the account of the empires in Daniel's visions by adding another empire that is a further embodiment of the beast. Their distinctive Christian angle is to present the story of Jesus as another, and climactic, intervention of the One on High who appears in Daniel 7. Like the visions in Daniel, these New Testament middle narratives describe this intervention as if it brings the ultimate End, but it does not do so. They recognize this point, in that they incorporate their own account of events that follow Jesus' death and resurrection and of situations that arise. They know that there will yet come the crisis that was historically constituted by the fall of Jerusalem, but that this crisis, too, will not be the End. The grand narrative they imply embraces creation, Abraham, Moses, Joshua, David; it embraces Assyria, Babylon, Medo-Persia and Greece; it embraces Rome and Jesus' birth, ministry, death and resurrection; it embraces the outpouring of God's Spirit, the proclamation of the gospel as far as Rome, the fall of Jerusalem and the End still to come.

THE ONGOING IMPORTANCE OF THE MIDDLE NARRATIVES

Considering this grand narrative when two thousand years have passed gives us a strangely new relationship with the middle narratives in both Testaments. If we had been living twenty or thirty years after Jesus, like Mark, then we might have thought that not much significance attaches to the earlier middle narratives, the ones in the First Testament, but the passing of two thousand years gives them more significance. In the West, at least, the church lives in a context more like the one Chronicles–Ezra–Nehemiah addresses and describes than the context of a Christian community in New Testament times. Our context is one in which God's promises have been partially fulfilled but in which nothing much seems now to be happening. We might even see ourselves as living in a situation like that of Judah in the exile. In some parts of the world and during some periods of history, the church finds itself living in a context more like the one addressed in Daniel's visions. The church in (say) Kenya in the 1950s might well find great encouragement in the middle narrative that pictures the rule of superpowers as not destined to go on forever.[28] While we would be unwise to live in light of one of those earlier middle narratives as if the events related in the later ones had not happened, the church's greater danger is to live as if it makes no difference that we are living two thousand years after the events that read as if they are bringing the scriptural grand narrative to its climax. To put the point more sharply, Isaiah 52 declares that God's reign has arrived, but the world did not change as much as you might have expected. Jesus said that God's reign has arrived, but we have noted in chapter two that the world did not change as much as you might have expected.

I am especially interested in the kind of biblical theology that involves creating from the varied materials within the Scriptures the big picture that might emerge from the whole, or using the building blocks constituted by this varied material to construct an edifice that makes good use of them all and doesn't involve either the importing of further materials from elsewhere or the casting aside of some of the materials in the conviction that they don't really belong in this building. But it also involves discerning which materials need highlighting in order to articulate the statement that needs making in the context in which the building is to be erected and to function. The First Testament middle narratives look especially significant in this connection.

---

[28]Just after I first drafted this chapter, the British government agreed to pay substantial compensation to Kenyan victims of torture at the hands of the British colonial administration in those times.

- 5 -

How People Have
Mis(?)read Hebrews[1]

There is a contrast between the relative neglect of Hebrews in biblical scholarship and its profound effect on Christian thinking over the centuries. In this
chapter I focus on the way it has affected Christian understanding of the First
Testament: not its exegetical method, but its hermeneutics and the influence
of its interpretation of the First Testament. Much of that influence has been
negative. This fact is not exactly its fault; Hebrews has significant positive
implications for Christian thinking about the First Testament, but these have
been less influential. Hebrews has had two chief negative side effects on
Christian reading of the First Testament, arising from the way it speaks of
sacrifice and the way it uses First Testament figures as models of faith.

Sacrifice and Sin

In Christian thinking it goes without saying that the First Testament sees
sacrifice as the necessary way Israelites got right with God. It thus follows the
declaration in Hebrews, "Without bloodshed there is no remission of sin"
(Heb 9:22). Hebrews makes that point in the course of using sacrifice as a way
of understanding the significance of Jesus' death. The ultimate way we get
right with God is that, in dying, Jesus offered himself as a sacrifice for us; it
is on that basis that we find forgiveness.

There is a contrast between the appeal in Hebrews to sacrifice and the way

---

[1]See Jon C. Laansma, "Hebrews: Yesterday, Today and Future," in *Christology, Hermeneutics, and
Hebrews*, ed. Jon C. Laansma and Daniel J. Treier (New York: T & T Clark, 2012), pp. 1-32 (pp. 1-2).

the First Testament speaks. The First Testament makes little or no link between sacrifice and sin or forgiveness. In the First Testament as elsewhere, sacrifice is a religious practice with a wide variety of meanings, like other religious actions such as standing or kneeling or raising one's hands. The First Testament rarely makes the meaning of sacrifice explicit, though in the systematic instructions about sacrifice in Leviticus 1–7 several features are noteworthy. First, there is no reference to sin in these instructions regarding the regular sacrifices, the burnt offerings, grain offerings and fellowship offerings. The instructions for the burnt offering do make one reference to its capacity to make expiation, but most First Testament references to burnt offerings do not suggest that expiation is its main significance.[2] For the fellowship offering, the traditional translation of zebaḥ shĕlāmîm is "peace-offering," which could give the impression that the sacrifice related to obtaining reconciliation with God, but even a traditional commentary such as Matthew Henry's recognizes that it does not have this significance.[3] In modern translations "sacrifice of well-being" is the chief alternative to "fellowship-offering" as a rendering of zebaḥ shĕlāmîm. Leviticus spells out three reasons for making this offering (Lev 7:11-18). It can be an expression of thankfulness for some blessing, such as the birth of a child. It can be offered in fulfillment of a promise: for instance, a promise made in connection with a prayer for healing. Or it can be a "freewill offering," made voluntarily, simply because a person wants to do so. In none of these connections is it anything to do with sin.

Following on the general instructions about burnt offerings, grain offerings and fellowship offerings in Leviticus 1–3 are instructions regarding two further sacrifices, which have been traditionally designated the sin offering and the guilt offering, but the kind of sins and guilt that these relate to are largely accidental infringements of the rules that bring uncleanness on an individual or on the community. They are not designed to deal with deliberate sin. A person cannot bring one of these offerings in order to get right with God in connection with worshiping another god or making an image or working on the Sabbath or committing adultery. In such circumstances, all you can do is repent and cast yourself on God's mercy, as is recognized in

---

[2]See, e.g., the discussion in Jacob Milgrom, *Leviticus 1–16* (New York: Doubleday, 1991), pp. 174-77.
[3]See *Matthew Henry's Commentary on the Whole Bible* (reprinted Wilmington, DE: Sovereign Grace, 1972) on Lev 3.

prayers such as Psalm 51 or Lamentations. Your hope then is that God may "carry" your sin—the literal meaning of the verb most commonly translated "forgive," the verb *nāśā'*. We have noted in chapter one that carrying someone's sin implies accepting responsibility for it instead of making the other person do so. To put it another way, your hope is that God may pay the price for your sin in this way, because he is a person full of compassion and mercy. No sacrifice on the part of the sinful person is involved. God's willingness to carry responsibility for human sin and pay the price for it comes to its apogee in his willingness to let humanity kill his Son, and then to raise him from death. God thereby sacrifices himself for humanity. Hebrews thus uses the familiar imagery of sacrifice to help readers understand the way Jesus' death puts things right between humanity and God.

TYPOLOGY

Its way of making this link has come to be called typological. Typological thinking assumes (first) an analogy between God's acts in two contexts, it assumes (second) a process whereby a physical, material act in the first context becomes a metaphor in the second context and it assumes (third) that the second act involves a heightening of what God did in the second context. So first, there is an analogy between what happened in Israelite worship through an animal's death and what happened through Christ's death; second, the former is a literal sacrifice, the latter a metaphorical one; and third, what Christ's death achieves is much more telling than what the animal's death achieves.

Typological thinking thus makes it possible to connect some new reality and an earlier reality. The link illumines the new reality, but it doesn't necessarily thereby establish the intrinsic meaning of the earlier reality. To put it another way, types are perceived only with hindsight. Nothing in the First Testament suggests that sacrifice was a type of something to happen in the future. Putting things right between humanity and God is not the meaning of sacrifice in itself. It is not the case that God inspired the sacrificial system so that people would understand Jesus' death. God did inspire Leviticus to adapt the conventional sacrificial system of a traditional society, so that it would work within faith in Yahweh in a way that could express faith in Yahweh and offer him worship and thanksgiving. And God did then inspire

Hebrews to use its framework because its readers knew it.[4] The argument of Hebrews is that if God's purpose in our lives could have reached completion (*teleiōsis*) through the work of the Levitical priesthood, there would have been no need of another priesthood (Heb 7:11). The old regulation is set aside because it was weak and useless in that it could bring nothing to completion, and a better hope is introduced whereby we can draw near to God (Heb 7:18-19). So it forms an aspect of a better covenant (Heb 7:22).

The argument thus works backward. It does not start from a sense on the part of Jews that the Levitical system did not work. It starts from the fact that Jesus is the one who brings God's purpose to its fulfillment, and it illustrates the point by extrapolating back to the inadequacy of the Levitical system. To that end, the Levitical system is being evaluated on a basis different from the one upon which it was given. The evaluation may presuppose that there were people who thought you could get to "completion" through keeping the law, which the Torah itself does not suggest.

One can imagine that this way of communicating the significance of Jesus' death was effective in relation to Jews and others who were familiar with sacrifice, though elsewhere in the New Testament sacrifice is nowhere near as common as a model for understanding Jesus' death as it is in Hebrews. Conversely, the New Testament makes use of the metaphor of sacrifice in connections other than explaining the significance of Jesus' execution. Romans, for instance, speaks of believers offering themselves to God as a living sacrifice, and of the Gentiles becoming an offering acceptable to God (Rom 12:1-2; 15:16). The New Testament as a whole thus reflects the broadness of the significance of sacrifice in the First Testament.

In a later Christian context, the focus on the way sacrifice can illumine the significance of Jesus' death has two disadvantages. One is that people are no longer familiar with sacrifice. The practice that was well-known and therefore provided an illuminating metaphor is now unfamiliar, so that it becomes an obstacle rather than an aid. In order to help people understand Jesus' death as a sacrifice, one first has to explain sacrifice. But doing so removes the point about the metaphor, which lay in its familiarity. It involves trying to explain

---

[4]Cf. Stephen R. Holmes's comments, "Death in the Afternoon," in *The Epistle to the Hebrews and Christian Theology*, ed. Richard Bauckham et al. (Grand Rapids: Eerdmans, 2009), pp. 229-52 (p. 249).

something difficult by means of something even more difficult. The other disadvantage, which is my more immediate concern, is that this focus on linking sacrifice to sin has skewed Christian understanding of First Testament sacrifice. One consequential further snag is that it frees Christian worship to be cheap and emotional and rationalistic, whereas the model offered by the First Testament is of worship that is costly and involves the whole person. Sacrifice can vividly express commitment, thankfulness, penitence and reparation.

MODELS OF FAITH

The other unfortunate side effect of Hebrews's use of the First Testament is that it has issued in a skewing of the way Christians look at the stories of people such as Abel, Enoch, Noah, Abraham and the other figures who appear in Hebrews 11. No doubt we should not blame Hebrews for that result of reading it, any more than blame Hebrews or John's Gospel for the anti-Judaism that has been read out of them. And there are ways in which we may be grateful for Hebrews 11. Whereas modern Christians are embarrassed by the violence of some First Testament heroes, Hebrews feels no such embarrassment about these people who "conquered kingdoms . . . , became powerful in battle and routed foreign armies" (Heb 11:33-34). Hebrews makes it impossible to argue that the New Testament would disapprove of the violence of the First Testament.

But these stories, and the other First Testament stories to which Hebrews refers, were not designed to provide examples of faith in action, examples for other people to follow, which is the way Hebrews has been understood. Further, Genesis does not say that Abel's offering was acceptable because it was offered in faith, nor that Enoch pleased God by faith, nor that Noah acted on the basis of faith. I do not question that they did so, but Genesis does not say it, for the significant reason that Genesis is not concerned with providing stories about people who provide human examples for other people to follow. Genesis is an account of God's relationship with the world, not of people's response to God.

As is the case with its use of the First Testament material on sacrifice, Hebrews is taking up First Testament material in order to explicate its own point. It wants to drive its readers forward in their life of faith, and it appeals to the Genesis stories to illustrate its theme. Indeed, it's been argued that the immediate purpose of Hebrews 11 is not to urge faith on its readers but to exalt Jesus, whose faith was even greater.[5] Hebrews is often said to do theology by reading Scripture. But in doing so it operates like much modern theological interpretation, by bringing in convictions from outside the scriptural text and expounding the text in light of those convictions rather than attending to the Scriptures' own agenda.[6]

In a later Christian context such as our own, its interpretation has again facilitated a skewing of Christian reading of the First Testament, which commonly assumes that stories about First Testament characters are designed to provide us with positive or negative examples. Actually, the First Testament is more about God than about us, as is Hebrews. It thinks we need to become aware of God's ways in the world, and this conviction explains its telling the stories that it does, and the way it tells them. If anyone is the spiritual and ethical model in the Torah, it is God, not some human being. "Be holy like me" (Lev 19:1), the Torah says, not "Be holy like Abraham or Moses."

My two examples together show the negative results of the Christian assumption that the New Testament provides a hermeneutic for the First Testament. Christians have commonly worked with that assumption, and Christian scholars have either sought to explain why they shouldn't do so or have sought to show that the New Testament has a hermeneutic that modern Christians can understand and accept. Our problem lies in modern assumptions about what counts as proper interpretation. The New Testament shows that God often chooses to use intuitive interpretations that enable a text to speak to a new question in a way that has little or nothing to do with the text's intrinsic meaning, and God does the same in many Christians' experience. Some discernment will be required if we are to determine whether such an interpretation does come from God. But the fact that an interpretation does not have much link with the text's own meaning does not rule out this possibility.

The First Testament's horizon needs to be allowed to broaden and correct the preunderstanding with which Christians come to the First Testament from the New Testament. It is not that the New Testament is wrong but that

---

[5]So Christopher A. Richardson in *Pioneer and Perfecter of Faith* (Tübingen: Mohr, 2012).
[6]See Andrew T. Lincoln, "Hebrews and Biblical Theology," in *Out of Egypt: Biblical Theology and Biblical Interpretation*, ed. Craig Bartholomew et al. (Grand Rapids: Zondervan, 2004), pp. 313-38 (pp. 330-31). Cf. Luke Timothy Johnson, "The Scriptural World of Hebrews," *Interpretation* (2003): 237-50.

the significance of its own use of the First Testament has been misunderstood. It was not providing us with a lens through which we should now interpret the First Testament. It was not doing exegesis. It was applying Scripture to its own questions. To put it more paradoxically, the hermeneutical guidance that the New Testament offers us is that we should not be looking to it for hermeneutical guidance, unless the guidance is an invitation to be imaginative in seeking to see how First Testament texts speak to our concerns. Apart from that, our First Testament hermeneutic comes from the First Testament itself, which implicitly asks us to interpret it in light of the way it spoke about God and us to the people for whom it was written and for whom it was accepted as Scripture.[7]

THE NEW, BETTER COVENANT

Poignantly, there is a converse point to be made about Hebrews's use of the First Testament. I could wish that this other aspect had been as influential as the first. It is that Hebrews rightly sees the church as in a position in relation to God that is analogous to Israel's, uses the First Testament in a way that reflects this assumption, and thereby sets a more promising example to us, but an example of which we have taken less notice.

My point involves recognizing a paradox within Hebrews itself. It declares that the new covenant of which Jeremiah spoke has been established, through Jesus (Heb 8:7-13; 10:15-18). Yet a moment's reflection confirms that this statement involves some oversimplification. The new covenant was to effect the writing of God's revelation into people's minds, with the result that they no longer needed to teach each other. Thus another of the contrasts between the Testaments that I listed in the introduction to this volume is that God's teaching is now written into our minds rather than written only on stone. Yet the very existence and contents of Hebrews show that God's revelation is not written into people's minds.[8] Hebrews addresses an audience that needs basic instructions on matters such as love, hospitality, faithfulness in marriage, contentment and the role of their leaders in teaching them (Heb 13:1-25). Those instructions are not far from being a restatement of the Ten Commandments. The instruction that the audience needs is basic indeed. People

---

[7]See further chapter nine below.
[8]Cf. Craig R. Koester, *Hebrews* (New York: Doubleday, 2001), p. 112.

who have experienced that of which Jeremiah 31 speaks would not be vulnerable to the comment about needing their faculties to be trained to distinguish good and evil (Heb 5:14).[9] Whatever new potential there is in Jeremiah's new covenant, it is not realized in the congregation that Hebrews addresses, nor in other New Testament congregations such as that at Corinth. Nor does the church today look like an embodiment of the new covenant. In this sense, the new covenant has surely not been established.

There is a converse point. Jeremiah 31:31-34 was a promise made to Israel on the verge of the fall of Jerusalem or during the exile. It would not be particularly good news to its hearers if it was destined for fulfillment only six centuries later. Indeed, it did not wait six centuries. Within a few decades, there was again a worshiping community in Jerusalem living as Yahweh's people with Yahweh as their God, one that in due course showed itself to be a community with quite a lot of the Torah written into its minds—people no longer worshiped other gods, made images,[10] neglected the Sabbath and so on. I don't know that they avoided adultery or covetousness, but then, neither does the church in the New Testament, or today.[11]

The fact that the new covenant has not been effectively implemented in the church means that we are not in so different a situation from that of Israel. Our lives do not look to be morally superior to Israel's, nor do we seem to have a closer relationship with God than the one the First Testament speaks of. Hebrews itself speaks in this way in its telling exposition of Psalm 95. When it refers to the way the wilderness generation failed to enter God's rest, and goes on to take "rest" as an image for salvation in Christ, one might have expected it to be implying that the church has entered this rest, but in fact it urges people to make sure that they don't follow the wilderness generation's example. They could fail to enter this rest as that generation did,

[9]Mark D. Nanos, "*New* or Renewed Covenantalism?" in Bauckham et al., *The Epistle to the Hebrews and Christian Theology*, pp. 183-88 (p. 186).

[10]Ephraim Stern has noted how archaeological investigations have not found images or indications of the worship of other deities in Judahite areas in the Persian period, which contrasts sharply with the evidence for the period of the monarchy (see, e.g., "What Happened to the Cult Figurines?" *Biblical Archaeology Review* 15, no. 4 [July/August 1989]: 22-29, 53-54).

[11]Contrast the comment by Susanne Lehne, who suggests that "it is only when the prophecy is appropriated by Christians (and probably by the members of the Qumran community) for their own times that the problematic nature [of the promises in Jer 31:31-34] becomes apparent because of their failure to be realized" (*The New Covenant in Hebrews* [Sheffield: Sheffield Academic Press, 1990], p. 34).

and as in effect later generations of Israel could, notwithstanding their being physically in the land. Believers in Jesus are not in a less vulnerable position than Israel's. They are in the same position.

The exhortations in Hebrews 13 show that the problem here is not that Hebrews is unaware of the facts about the church that belie its declaration that the new covenant has been implemented. As is the case with the language of sacrifice, the concern in Hebrews is to help people understand the monumental implications of Jesus' death, and one might indeed say that Jesus has opened up the possibility of a new covenant, or has acted in such a way as to guarantee the implementing of a new covenant, for people who did not benefit from what Yahweh did in the sixth and succeeding centuries— people such as Gentiles like most Christian readers. It is worth noting that Paul also quotes Jeremiah 31:31-34, in Romans 11:27, and does so in connection with what God will do at the End, not what God has already done.

Perhaps we should simply not be too punctilious in interpreting Hebrews's quotation from Jeremiah 31. Each time it repeats the quotation, it closes with God's promise not to remember Israel's sins, and the focus of its exposition of what Jesus has done lies here. Hebrews includes the promise from Jeremiah that God will write the Torah into people's minds, but it does not make any more reference to this promise. The interest of Hebrews lies in the way what Jesus has achieved is "better" than what the Torah speaks of, as is suggested by its beginning with the declaration that Jesus is better than the angels (Heb 1:4). So how is what Jesus achieved "better"? A significant element in the answer is that Jesus introduces "a better hope with which we draw near to God," a hope based on a "better covenant" that brings a salvation such as will last forever, because he always lives to intercede for us—a better covenant because it is enacted on better promises (Heb 7:19, 22, 25; 8:6; so also the further occurrences of the word *better* in Heb 10:34; 11:16, 35, 40; 12:24).

THE EMBODIED REVELATION

A similar implication emerges from the exhortation in Hebrews 12. The chapter reminds readers that they have not come to a frightening physical mountain burning with fire, but to the heavenly Jerusalem. Another of the student perceptions about the relationship between the Testaments that I quoted in the introduction to this volume contrasted real access to God

through Christ with purely bodily access under the old covenant, and referred to Hebrews 12:18-24. But the First Testament makes clear that people
had real access to God under the old covenant. One's response to the account of a relationship with God that is offered in the Psalms or in the stories
of ordinary people such as Hannah is not, "If only they had the real relationship with God that I have after Jesus came," but, "If only I had the real
relationship with God that they had before Jesus came."

It makes sense to take Hebrews 12 to be referring to the objective difference
that Jesus' death and resurrection made over against the First Testament:
Jesus opened up the possibility of *eternal* salvation, which the First Testament
does not speak of.[12] The implication is then not that people can therefore relax
in a way that Moses could not. We are still to worship God with reverence
and awe, because it is still true that our God is a consuming fire. In this respect, once more we are in the same position as First Testament Israel.

There is a related observation to be made about the opening verses of
Hebrews. God spoke through the prophets in different times and many ways,
but then at the end of the days spoke through a Son. John Calvin comments
that where there was an "imperfection" about God's speaking through the
prophets, we now have a "fuller revelation."[13] John Webster adds that whereas
God spoke "through" the prophets, his message was therefore "an indirect
word, . . . not itself directly and immediately God's word"; hence what God
says through the prophets was characterized by "relativity and imperfection."[14]
Now Hebrews indeed affirms that God's speaking through Jesus was superior
to that through the prophets, but it does not say that it was fuller, nor that the
prophets' teaching was relative or imperfect, nor that it was less direct. Hebrews uses the same preposition *en* of God's speaking *through* the prophets
and *through* Jesus. The distinction it makes between the two revelations is
that the one is piecemeal and the other is embodied in one person, but it's the
same revelation. While the journey of God's pilgrim people is "irreversibly

---

[12]Cf. I. Howard Marshall, "Soteriology in Hebrews," in Bauckham et al., *The Epistle to the Hebrews and Christian Theology*, pp. 253-77 (pp. 268-69), following K. Grayston, *Dying, We Live* (Oxford: Oxford University Press, 1990), pp. 266-67; also Holmes, "Death in the Afternoon," pp. 239-46. See further the section on "Resurrection Hope" in chapter one above.

[13]John Calvin, *Commentaries on the Epistle of Paul the Apostle to the Hebrews* (reprinted Grand Rapids: Eerdmans, 1948), pp. 22-23.

[14]John Webster, "One Who Is Son," in Bauckham et al., *The Epistle to the Hebrews and Christian Theology*, pp. 69-94 (pp. 75-76).

enlightened" by Jesus, this people continues the same journey.[15] Jesus' death has issued in the annulling of specific commands within the terms of the old covenant (Heb 7:18), but not in the annulling of the covenant itself or of the instructions it gives for the people's life.[16]

So Hebrews speaks with two voices about our relationship with the old covenant and with the old covenant Scriptures. Graham Hughes long ago noted that the tension we have been examining is one between the theological-christological statements in Hebrews and the parenetic statements. The theological statements declare that Jesus has done something final and complete. The parenetic parts picture Christians standing "exactly where hearers of the Old Testament Word were placed (2.2f)."[17] Hughes implies that this analysis resolves the problem of this tension, but I am not sure it does so. Alexander Wedderburn has suggested that the way Hebrews talks about sacrifice saws off the branch on which it is sitting.[18] If Hebrews sees people as in a new theological situation but one that does not make a difference to their lives, is it not taking the same risk? Perhaps the way to approach the question is to appeal to deconstruction, which can have a positive significance for biblical interpretation. The Scriptures' theological statements can involve them in making strong assertions that risk oversimplification, and the reader needs to look for the concealed other truth that must modify the strong assertion, if one is seeking balance. But preachers and biblical writers, like prophets, often need to make unbalanced statements in order to get their point home.

It is regrettable that we have heard so loudly in Hebrews a voice that seemed to imply that the Scriptures associated with the old covenant and the physical Zion belong only to an earlier stage in the story of God's people, and that we have thereby done ourselves a disservice in our own self-understanding as well as encouraged anti-Judaism. It is regrettable that in picking up this aspect of Hebrews, we have missed its encouragement to listen to those Scriptures,

[15]Markus Bockmuehl, "Abraham's Faith in Hebrews 11," in Bauckham et al., *The Epistle to the Hebrews and Christian Theology*, pp. 364-73 (p. 369).

[16]Against Ernst Käsemann, *The Wandering People of God* (Minneapolis: Augsburg, 1984), p. 57. See further Barry C. Joslin, "Hebrews 7–10 and the Transformation of the Law," in *A Cloud of Witnesses*, ed. Richard Bauckham et al. (New York: T & T Clark, 2008), pp. 100-117 (p. 102); Clark M. Williamson, "Anti-Judaism in Hebrews?" *Interpretation* (2003): 266-79.

[17]Graham Hughes, *Hebrews and Hermeneutics* (Cambridge: Cambridge University Press, 1979), pp. 68-69.

[18]A. J. M. Wedderburn, "Sawing Off the Branches," *Journal of Theological Studies* 56 (2005): 393-414.

and deprived ourselves of the resource comprised by them.

I have not done my own work on the process whereby Hebrews came to be part of the New Testament, but the conventional wisdom says that for several centuries churches in the East accepted Hebrews, appreciating its significance for Christian pilgrimage, whereas churches in the West were more suspicious of it until they came to value its contribution to trinitarian thinking.[19] Conversely, churches in the West accepted the Revelation to John, but churches in the East came to accept it only later. It's almost as if the Eastern churches were saying, "We'll accept Revelation if you accept Hebrews," and the Western churches were saying, "We'll accept Hebrews if you accept Revelation." I wonder how history might have been different if the Eastern churches had given up Hebrews and the Western churches had given up Revelation? Christian faith in the United States (where much attention has been paid to aspects of Revelation) would certainly have been different, and so would Christian (mis)understanding of the First Testament.

I do assume that God's providence was involved in the decision the churches made. I'd just like to see an upending of the unbalanced way Hebrews has influenced interpretation of sacrifice and of First Testament characters, and a realization of the positive potential of Hebrews for an appreciation of the First Testament.

---

[19]See, e.g., Koester, *Hebrews*, pp. 19-27.

- 6 -

The Costly Loss of
First Testament Spirituality

As an expression of being imbued with the Spirit, Ephesians urges people
to speak to one another with psalms, hymns and spiritual songs, to sing
and make music to the Lord, and to give thanks to God for everything
(Eph 5:18-20). It goes on to urge them to pray in the Spirit, to keep on
praying for all the Lord's people and to pray for Paul to have the words and
the courage he needs in order to proclaim the revelation of the gospel (Eph
6:18-20). While songs like Mary's and Zechariah's (Lk 1:46-79) and other
praise songs in the New Testament indicate that the early church's praise
was not confined to the Psalms, they also indicate that this praise stood in
the tradition of the Psalms and followed their models. We noted in chapter
one that when Ephesians speaks of psalms, it may not have in mind only
the praise and prayer songs in the book of Psalms, but it surely includes
them. Placing Ephesians and the book of Psalms alongside each other invites the inference that the Psalms model the nature of worship, thanksgiving and prayer. Apparently we should not assume that we know how to
pray or that we can simply trust to the Spirit's direct inspiration. The
Psalms are in Scripture to guide our praise and prayer. If the Psalms are
where Christians always used to learn to pray,[1] the church has largely abandoned that model. When I listen to Christians pray, I hear little evidence
of our praying being shaped by them (or by any other part of Scripture,

---

[1]Cf. Eugene H. Peterson, *Working the Angles* (Grand Rapids: Eerdmans, 1995), p. 50. Dietrich Bonhoeffer offers a distinctive take on this point in *Life Together/Prayerbook of the Bible* (Minneapolis:
Fortress, 1996), pp. 53-58, 174-76.

including other prayers in Lamentations, Ezra–Nehemiah, and elsewhere). The loss of their influence is a costly one.

Worship

I used to describe what I do on Sundays as "leading worship," but the meaning of that expression has changed, along with the meaning of the word *awesome* (the two changes are not unrelated). Leading worship used to refer to the role of a pastor who would preside over a congregation's praising, praying, confessing, interceding and listening to Scripture. It now commonly refers (at least in the United States) to the role of a "worship minister" or "music minister," who presides over and facilitates a block of singing that occupies one of the two major parts of a service—the other being the sermon. The emaciated nature of what counts as worship is a feature of our culture.

This past Sunday the first reading prescribed by our church's lectionary happened to come from Jeremiah 2:

Yahweh has said this:
What wrongdoing did your ancestors find in me,
  that they went far away from me?
They went after emptiness and became emptiness,
  and didn't say, "Where is Yahweh,
The one who brought us up from the country of Egypt
  and enabled us to go through the wilderness,
Through a country of steppe and pit,
  a country of drought and deep darkness,
A country through which no one passed
  and where no human being lived?"
I enabled you to come into a country of farmland
  to eat its fruit and its good things.
But you came and defiled my country;
  you made my possession an outrage.
The priests didn't say, "Where is Yahweh?,"
  the people controlling the Teaching didn't acknowledge me.
The shepherds rebelled against me,
  the prophets prophesied by Ba'al
  and followed beings that couldn't achieve anything.
Therefore I shall contend with you more (Yahweh's declaration),

and contend with your grandchildren.
Because cross over to the shores of Cyprus and see,
    send off to Qedar and observe well,
    see if something like this has happened.
Has a nation changed its gods,
    when those are not gods?
But my people have changed my splendor
    for what doesn't achieve anything.
Be devastated at this, heavens,
    shudder, be utterly desolate (Yahweh's declaration).
Because my people have done two bad things:
    they've abandoned me, the fountain of running water,
To dig themselves cisterns,
    breakable cisterns, that can't hold water.

People sometimes speak of the church in the United States as being in exile. That assessment seems quaint to someone from Europe—if you want to see what a church in exile looks like, look there. The church in the United States is weaker and less influential than it used to be, and it's subject to attack, but Jerusalem has not fallen yet. We are rather living at a moment like Jeremiah's in the decades before the exile, and Jeremiah's analysis of Judah's situation is transferable to ours.[2]

WHAT WORSHIP HAS LOST

Jeremiah asks the question, "Why are we in a reduced state, why are we a shadow of our former self?" The first reason is that they have forgotten their gospel, the good news, the story of what God did for them, the story about the God who brought them out of Egypt and gave them the land; and they have not asked where God was when things went south. The second reason is that they have given up on God's written word. "The people controlling the Teaching, the Torah, didn't acknowledge me," Yahweh says. The written word of God was not shaping their relationship with God, and their lives. Instead, third, they have turned to other spiritual resources. They have abandoned the fountain of running water, in order to dig themselves cisterns that can't hold water. The

---

[2]This section on Jeremiah adapts material from my paper "As a Commentator, One Might Ask, 'What Would Jeremiah or John Say?'" to appear in a festschrift in 2015.

best water supply would be a spring or well from which people can get fresh water, but sometimes people would have to make do with a tank to collect water in the winter for use during the summer. A leak in the tank then has deathly implications. How stupid to give up a spring and choose to rely on a tank, specifically a leaky tank? Yet Israel has done so in turning from Yahweh.

It happened because they thought the culture around them had the answer to their key needs, and they assimilated to the culture in their turning to Ba'al as a deity who could meet their needs. Perhaps they continued to call God *Yahweh*, but they had so changed Yahweh's nature to that of Ba'al that in effect Ba'al was the one they were worshiping.

Parallel factors can affect the church. It can assimilate to its culture, and worship is a key way in which it does so. Worship becomes the way we deal with our emptiness and isolation. Worship is designed to make us feel good. The point about God is to make us feel good. So churches may give up the reading of Scripture in worship, because the reading of Scripture is not very engaging. They may give up much reference to the gospel story, because those events happened a long time ago and don't look as if they speak directly to people's lives. So it is possible to go through a whole worship service without hearing any reference to the gospel events—to the way God created the world, delivered Israel, sent Jesus to live and die for us, and raised him from the dead. Like Israel, we can forget the gospel and give up on God's written word because we are so concerned with our personal needs.

What we really need is to be brought out of ourselves by seeing our lives set in the context of a bigger picture, a bigger story, the gospel story (in the context of this book, it will be clear that by the gospel story I mean the whole story that comes to a climax in Jesus but that is not confined to his story). Yet we are so overwhelmed by our emptiness, isolation and insignificance that we don't pay attention to this bigger story. All we want inside church as outside church is to think about ourselves in our need. So we turn God into someone whose focus is on meeting those needs. In worship we use many of the same words our forebears used, the words *God* and *Lord* and *Jesus*, but the content we read into them comes from the contemporary context. We are scratching where we itch. But when people have a serious itch, they need more than scratching to put it right. We are trying to short-circuit the process whereby God gives content and meaning to our lives. We make God a quick fix for our needs. But quick fixes don't work. The only fix that works is the gospel story and the Scriptures where we find that story. But in worship we have given up on those.

We have devised a religion to enable us to give expression to our individual sad selves and we hope it will make us feel better, but it doesn't really do so. We may leave worship on a high but we are soon just as sad as when we arrived. We think that more of the same is the solution. If we make the worship livelier, it will work. But we're trying to get a drink from a tank with no water. We have focused on our immediate felt needs and given up on the gospel story that made us what we are. We are focused on ourselves, rather than on God, on Scripture, on the church, on the gospel and on our calling on God. We have assimilated to the culture, as Israel did, and forgotten the big picture. We think the gospel is just about ourselves and God—especially about ourselves. The worship the Psalms commend and model is one that focuses on God.

Testimony

Once every month or so, I sit in front of the congregation instead of preaching, we reread one of the Scripture lessons together and I ask people whether there was a verse that jumped off the page for them (our congregation numbers only thirty or forty, so it is a practicable procedure). The second passage of Scripture that we read in church last Sunday came from Hebrews 13, and we looked at this passage together. Almost before I had asked the question about what had jumped off the page, a woman came out with some of the lines from the chapter:

> He has said, "I will never leave you or forsake you." So we say with confidence,
> "The Lord is my helper; I will not be afraid. What can anyone do to me?" . . .
> Jesus Christ is the same yesterday and today and forever.[3]

We knew the tough year she had been through as the victim of abuse and fraud. Our knowledge gave great power to her testimony about God's presence with her and God's proving that she did not need to be afraid. It's the kind of testimony that builds up the trust of other people in a congregation. We do have a time every week in worship when people have a chance to give thanks for things, but ironically, they rarely produce such testimony at that time. Yet when there is something special to testify to, it comes out.

---

[3]The internal quotations come from Deut 31 and Ps 118.

The woman's testimony fulfills the function of testimony psalms (e.g., Ps 30). They are usually termed thanksgiving psalms, and they do give thanks, but they characteristically interweave thanksgiving addressed to God with testimony addressed to the other people in the congregation. They commonly tell a story along the lines of the one presupposed by that woman's testimony, a story of how things were okay, and how things collapsed one way or another, and how the person prayed and how God answered. It might seem puzzling that Ephesians 5:19 speaks of singing to one another with psalms, hymns and spiritual songs (cf. Col 3:16), but one clue to the rationale for such a way of speaking comes here. Our worship, and specifically our thanksgiving, addresses other people as well as God. It builds them up.

There is a paradoxical or an ironic extra comment to be made about praise and testimony. Israelite worship was costly. Whereas we can go to church with empty hands and expect to leave having received something, Israelites often went to worship taking the best lamb from their flock or bull from their herd. A Jebusite once had David show up at his threshing floor wanting to buy it to build a sanctuary there. Wisely guessing which way the wind might be blowing, he offered David the threshing floor as a gift, but David declined, declaring, "I will not offer up to Yahweh my God burnt offerings that cost me nothing" (1 Chron 21:24). Christians are inclined to think that their no longer having any obligation to offer sacrifices to God marks their faith as superior to that of the First Testament. At the very least, things are more complicated than that inference implies. Ironically, Jeremiah (like some other prophets) told people that Yahweh loathed their sacrifices—they thought that sacrifices pleased God whether or not their lives outside worship matched who Yahweh is. In our context, Jeremiah's message would be the opposite. He would be expecting us to find ways of offering God worship that cost us something, like the woman who put her last two dollars in the offertory (Lk 21:1-4).

PROTEST AND CONFESSION

The phrase I use as the title of this chapter comes from an article, "The Costly Loss of Lament."[4] In 1945, a nineteen-year-old German soldier called Jürgen

---

[4]Walter Brueggemann, *The Psalms and the Life of Faith* (Minneapolis: Fortress, 1995), pp. 98-111; the phrase was then taken up by Rolf Jacobson, "The Costly Loss of Praise," *Theology Today* 57 (2000): 375-85.

Moltmann was taken prisoner by the British and eventually placed in a camp in Sherwood Forest, not far from the seminary where I used to teach. There the Nottingham YMCA set him going on the theological study that eventually took him to being one of the great twentieth-century theologians. Having lived through the horrors of the Second World War, the collapse of an empire and its institutions, and the guilt and shame of their nation, many German prisoners collapsed inwardly and gave up all hope, some of them dying. "The same thing almost happened to me," Moltmann says, were it not for a "rebirth to a new life" that turned Christian faith into reality rather than formality. The experience of misery and forsakenness and daily humiliation gradually built up into an experience of God.

> It was the experience of God's presence in the dark night of the soul: "If I make my bed in hell, behold, thou art there." A well-meaning army chaplain had given me a New Testament. I thought it was out of place. I would rather have had something to eat. But then I became fascinated by the Psalms (which were printed in an appendix) and especially by Psalm 39: "I was dumb with silence, I held my peace, even from good; and my sorrow was stirred" (but the German is much stronger—"I have to eat up my grief within myself") . . . "Hold thou not thy peace at my tears: for I am a stranger with thee, and a sojourner, as all my fathers were." These psalms gave me the words for my own suffering. They opened my eyes to the God who is with those "that are of a broken heart."[5]

Claus Westermann speaks in similar terms about his own wartime experience, when the Psalms were the part of the Bible that most resonated with him (he then focused on the Psalms for a significant part of his academic career).

> I realized that the people who had written and prayed the psalms understood prayer differently than we do. Prayer was closer to life, closer to the reality in which they lived, than is true with us. For us, prayer is something a person does or is admonished to do—a human act. But in the Psalter, crying to God grows out of life itself; it is a reaction to the experiences of life, a cry from the heart.[6]

The Psalms invite us to let church be the place where you can talk about things that you can't talk about anywhere else.[7] We may be more inclined to view

---

[5] Jürgen Moltmann, *Experiences of God* (London: SCM, 1980), pp. 6-9. I have adapted these two paragraphs from my *Praying the Psalms* (Bramcote, UK: Grove, 1993).
[6] Claus Westermann, "The Bible and the Life of Faith," *Word and World* 13 (1993): 337-44 (340).
[7] I owe this phrase to a lecture by Walter Brueggemann at St. John's College, Nottingham.

church as a place where we can shut those things outside for an hour—but we then discover that they are still real when we leave church. I recall a scene in a movie or sitcom in which one girl is telling her friend about a problem. The friend asks her if she has told her therapist about the problem. "Oh no, it's personal," she replies. She hadn't got the point about therapy, in a way that we often don't get the point about church. The Psalms invite Israel to get this point about their prayer in the temple, or in their local sanctuary, or in their homes (most Israelites lived too far away from Jerusalem to pray there, so I guess they prayed mostly in those other contexts). The significance of the psalms of lament or psalms of protest (which seems to me a better description) has come home to many people over the past twenty or thirty years, and enabled them to find some freedom in prayer and protest. It would not be surprising if they have also thus found some maturity, given that Jesus, "the paradigm case of the truly human,"[8] during his time on earth "offered pleas and petitions to the one who was able to save him from death, with loud shouting and tears. . . . He learned obedience through the things he suffered" and thus was "made mature" (Heb 5:7-9).

It's an odd feature of these psalms that they rarely focus on the waywardness of the person praying. If they talk about a failure to keep covenant commitment, it's likely to be God's failure, not theirs. They thereby indicate the assumption that in order to pray in the manner they do, people need to be able to claim that they are basically committed to God's ways. This claim can make Western Christians feel uncomfortable. We are more used to being pressed to acknowledge that we are sinners. Yet if our lives are not characterized by a basic commitment of this kind, it's that fact that we need to talk to God about (and that fact rather than the minor peccadilloes that we may be more easily willing to acknowledge).

Intercession

There is another aspect of the protest psalms that troubles people and gives food for thought.

This year is the tenth anniversary of the partial genocide of the Darfuri people in Sudan, which involved the death of several hundred thousand people. Many of the Darfuri who escaped that atrocity, perhaps another two

---

[8]Anthony C. Thiselton, *The Hermeneutics of Doctrine* (Grand Rapids: Eerdmans, 2007), pp. 241, 242.

hundred thousand, fled to Chad and have been living in refugee camps there ever since. My stepdaughter Katie-Jay and her husband Gabriel have spent most of these ten years seeking to get the West to recognize the plight of the Darfuri and to take some action on their behalf. When I married Katie-Jay's mother, Kathleen, three years ago, we started making prayer for the Darfuri part of our prayer routine. When we are home for dinner, we use the Episcopal form of prayer for early evening before we eat, and we added to it a psalm that we said on behalf of the Darfuri people. We started at the beginning of the Psalter, and simply prayed the psalms one after each other, one a day.

The idea came from my own previous experience of praying the Psalms. Before I came to the United States, I taught in a Church of England seminary, where we were in prayer and worship every day. We followed the Church of England lectionary for the reading of Scripture, and we read through the Psalms one by one. We were not choosing a psalm to read each day on the basis of its corresponding to our current situation. We were reading (say) Psalm 47 because we read Psalm 46 yesterday and we would read Psalm 48 tomorrow. That practice made me ask what on earth we were doing, and I came to two conclusions. One was that by reading the entire Psalter we were shaping our habit of thinking about praise and prayer. The other was that in praying prayers or praises that did not correspond to our own circumstances, we were identifying with other parts of the Christian community and the world community whose circumstances corresponded to those out of which the psalm prayed. In other words, we were involved in intercession.

This realization provided me with an answer to another question about the Psalms that had puzzled me. It seemed obvious that the Psalms modeled the nature of supplication—of praying for oneself. But how did the First Testament community pray for other people—how did it intercede? There are hardly any explicitly intercessory prayers in the Psalter. There are only a few elsewhere in the First Testament, but a feature of some of them, particularly in the Prophets, is that the prayer takes first-person form. Someone is praying for other people, but is identifying with them: praying not for *them*, but for *us*. The intercession involved putting oneself in other people's place. This practice fits with the fact that etymologically *intercession* links with intervention and involves acting as a "go-between." Intercession implies interposing between two parties so as to bring them together. It entails identifying with one party and representing it to another. For a prophet, intercessory prayer involved identifying with people and representing them before God, so that one speaks as "we" or "I," not as "they" or "he" or "she." I realized that the apparent absence of intercessory prayers from the Psalter might mean that actually the "I" and "we" psalms could be used as intercessions as well as supplications. Perhaps Israel used them that way; certainly we might do so. In praying protest psalms, one need not be praying for oneself.

Specifically, in praying the prayers in the Psalms that speak out of oppression, affliction, persecution and tyranny, we pray not directly for ourselves but for people who experience oppression, affliction, persecution and tyranny, with whom we identify. We pray for God to put down tyrants and oppressors. In connection with the Darfuri, one might think of President Omar al-Bashir of Sudan, for whose arrest the International Criminal Court has issued a warrant on counts of war crimes, crimes against humanity and genocide.

A feature of the Psalms is then that they virtually never speak of taking violent action to put down oppressors (the major exception is some royal psalms that assume that God works via the human king in putting down resistance to God in the world). They do not give reasons for this omission. I am tempted to describe the Psalter as the most pacifist book in the Bible, though I try to resist the temptation because speaking in terms of pacifism is anachronistic; pacifism implies a framework of thinking that does not appear in either Testament.[9] I suspect that two other considerations underlie the stance of the Psalms. One is the simple practicality that the people who prayed the Psalms were usually in no position to take action against their oppressors. Prayer was all they had. But what a powerful weapon they knew it was! That fact links with the other consideration. Prophets such as Isaiah frequently insist that the vocation of the people of God is to trust God for their destiny and not to take action to safeguard it. The stance of the Psalms fits with that emphasis. "Praying the Psalms is an audacious act of trust."[10]

---

[9]It has been argued that the Essenes were pacifist, but the chief evidence seems to be Philo's statement that they were not involved in the manufacture of weapons (*Quod omnis probus liber sit* 78): see Joan E. Taylor, "Philo of Alexandria on the Essenes," *The Studia Philonica Annual* 19 (2007): 1-28 (15), where she also notes that Josephus (*Jewish War* 2.125) says that the Essenes carried weapons for self-protection, which implies they were not pacifist.

[10]David Augsburger, "Foreword," in *Praying Curses*, by Daniel M. Nehrbass (Eugene, OR: Pickwick, 2013), pp. ix-xii (p. x).

PRAYING AGAINST THE SUPERPOWER

The imprecatory Psalms, then, provide people who are oppressed with a means of urging God to take action against evil in the world, and they give people who identify with the oppressed a means of praying for them. It may well be that there is a therapeutic value in expressing anger, though it is also possible that expressing anger may only feed the flame.[11] Perhaps the question is whether the anger has truly been given to God. But the main point about imprecation is not to get things off one's chest so that one feels better, but to urge God to take action (compare Paul's comment in Rom 12:19).

In this connection it is possible that the imprecatory psalms are more significant for the brothers and sisters of the oppressed than for the oppressed themselves. The First Testament includes the awareness that people who are wronged may recognize a call to turn the other cheek and not desire the punishment of the people who have wronged them. Joseph takes that stance. Thus Zephania Kameeta's reworked version of Psalm 137, prayed in the midst of Namibia's struggle for independence from South Africa, asks that the apartheid system may be smashed on the rock, but not that white South African politicians may have that experience.[12] It may then be the responsibility of people who care about the victims of wrongdoing and who care about the vindication of right in the world to pray for God to put wrongdoers down and deliver their victims. The imprecatory psalms are for us to pray, who are not victims. Indeed, if we do not want to pray them, it raises questions about the shallowness of our own spirituality, theology and ethics. Do we not want to see wrongdoers put down and punished?

One reason for our not wanting to see it happen is that we may be on the receiving end of the putting down. That possibility is raised by another contemporary use of the imprecatory psalms, by Rastafarians.

Rastafarianism emerged in Jamaica nearly a century ago. Among its many biblical influences, it has especially used the imprecatory psalms in protesting against colonialism and in striving for national identity and social

---

[11]See the discussion in Dominick D. Hankle, "The Therapeutic Implications of the Imprecatory Psalms in a Christian Counseling Setting," *Journal of Psychology and Theology* 38 (2010): 275-80.
[12]See Zephania Kameeta, *Why, O Lord?* (Geneva: WCC, 1986), p. 48.

change. They were a "linguistic political tool to chant down the enemy."[13] "Babylon" comes to mean the West and its economic system.

The most notorious imprecatory psalm is 137, whose reggae version is called "Rivers of Babylon." It actually omits the closing verses that Western Christians find offensive, and replaces them by the closing line from Psalm 19 that asks for our words to be pleasing to God. I imagine the point of that last line is to underscore the prayer and urge God to respond to its plea for freedom. The song was written and first recorded in 1970 by a Jamaican band called The Melodians, but it was covered in 1978 by a slightly manufactured European-based group called Boney M.[14] This version was a long-running number-one record in Britain, though it was only a minor hit in the United States. Ironically, we British who listened to and sang the song never realized that it was about us, that we were Babylon. Perhaps the BBC would have banned it if we had realized.

Scholars in countries such as Britain and the United States are therefore wise to support the view of ordinary Christians that nobody should use such psalms. It would be dangerous if people prayed them and God listened and responded.

Christians commonly justify their opposition to the use of such psalms by suggesting that these psalms are out of keeping with the New Testament, but it is not so. While the New Testament doesn't quote Psalm 137, it does utilize imprecatory parts of Psalm 69 (e.g., Jn 2:17; Acts 1:20), which as a whole is more extensively imprecatory. Further, we noted in the introduction to this volume that Revelation 6:10 reports an imprecatory prayer on the part of the martyrs, who ask, "How long, Lord, holy and true, will you not judge and take redress for our blood from earth's inhabitants?" God's response is not to point out that such a prayer is inappropriate in light of Jesus' exhortation to forgive enemies; it is to promise them that the time will soon come. Since it has not done so, perhaps this promise provides further reason for praying in imprecatory fashion, or further reason for us Westerners to avoid doing so if we allow for the possibility that we will be its victims.

Jesus himself declares, "Woe to you, Korazin! Woe to you, Bethsaida!" for

---

[13]Nathaniel Samuel Murrell, "Tuning Hebrew Psalms to Reggae Rhythms," *Cross Currents* 50 (2000-2001): 525-40 (528). Murrell also edited (with William D. Spencer and Adrian Anthony McFarlane) the tellingly titled *Chanting Down Babylon* (Philadelphia: Temple University Press, 1998).

[14]Richard Middleton (who made helpful comments on a draft of my treatment of the imprecatory psalms) has drawn my attention to a more recent song based on the psalm by the Orthodox Jewish reggae/rap singer Matisyahu.

not responding to his teaching, and goes on to describe the terrible punishment that will come on the cities (Mt 11:21-24; cf., e.g., Mt 23:13-32). Paul declares curses on various people (1 Cor 16:22; Gal 1:8-9).[15] It looks as if Jesus and Paul want to see wrongdoers put down and punished, or at least that they affirm its necessity even if they also hope to forestall it by speaking in the way they do.

ALLEGORICAL INTERPRETATION

The New Testament thus suggests a critique of the comments of two well-known scholars who have been uncomfortable with Psalm 137. The first is C. S. Lewis, who wonders how a Christian can use the imprecatory psalms, and reverts to an allegorical approach:

> We know the proper object of utter hostility—wickedness, especially our own. . . . I can use even the horrible passage in 137 about dashing the Babylonian babies against the stones. I know things in the inner world which are like babies; the infantile beginnings of small indulgences, small resentments, which may one day become dipsomania [what we would call alcoholism] or settled hatred. . . . Against all such pretty infants . . . the advice of the Psalm is best. Knock the little bastards' brains out.[16]

There are many dangers in allegorical interpretation, and Lewis here illustrates several of them. Its problem is usually not that it leads us to make declarations that are in themselves out of keeping with the direct teaching of Scripture. It is that it enables us to avoid seeing what the Holy Spirit was inspiring in Scripture, in order rather to focus on something that we are more interested in. Our interest will often lie in matters of individual spirituality rather than our outward lives. It enables us to avoid seeing what God wants us to see.

Lewis published his *Reflections on the Psalms* in the 1950s, the decade when people from different parts of the British Empire (not least Jamaica) were being encouraged to immigrate into Britain to drive buses, work in factories and staff hospitals. The book came out two years before the speech in South Africa by Prime Minister Harold Macmillan about the "wind of change" blowing through Britain's empire in Africa.[17] There is a link between

---

[15]See further Nehrbass, *Praying Curses*, pp. 137-40.
[16]C. S. Lewis, *Reflections on the Psalms* (London: Bles, 1958; reprinted London: Collins, 1961), pp. 113-14.
[17]The text is widely available on the Internet in transcript and audio forms.

Lewis's avoidance of the literal meaning of Psalm 137 and the postcolonial implications of the psalm (as we would now put it), but an allegorical interpretation of the psalm avoids these implications.

The other scholar is David C. Steinmetz. In an article that has become a classic text for the interest in recovering the significance of precritical interpretation of Scripture, he speaks of the difficulty raised for Christians by Psalm 137 with its talk of baby bashing, difficulty raised by the fact that we are "expressly forbidden" to avenge ourselves on our enemies. "Unless Psalm 137 has more than one meaning," he says, "it cannot be used as a prayer by the Church and must be rejected as a lament belonging exclusively to the piety of ancient Israel." Allegorical interpretation, he goes on,

> made it possible for the church to pray directly and without qualification even a troubling Psalm like 137. After all, Jerusalem was not merely a city in the Middle East; it was, according to the allegorical sense, the church; according to the tropological sense, the faithful soul; and according to the anagogical sense, the center of God's new creation. The Psalm became a lament of those who long for the establishment of God's future kingdom and who are trapped in this disordered and troubled world, which with all its delights is still not their home. They seek an abiding city elsewhere. The imprecations against the Edomites and the Babylonians are transmuted into condemnations of the world, the flesh, and the devil. If you grant the fourfold sense of Scripture, David sings like a Christian.[18]

Steinmetz's comments stimulate several remarks. First, we have noted that the early church had no difficulty with psalms such as Psalm 137, understood in their literal sense. Second, the psalm makes no reference to avenging oneself on one's enemies. Indeed, its implication is the opposite. It is an expression of the regular First Testament inclination to leave vengeance to God. Third, one significance of the psalm is that it is a prayer by an oppressed people for God to judge an oppressor. We have noted that most modern biblical interpreters belong to oppressor nations rather than oppressed peoples; being able to rule out its literal meaning makes it possible for the psalm to have no purchase on us. An oppressed people's attitude to the psalm may be different. A fourth, related point is that what presents itself

---

[18]"The Superiority of Pre-Critical Exegesis," *Theology Today* 37 (1980): 27-38 (29-30, 30-31); cf. Daniel J. Treier, *Introducing Theological Interpretation of Scripture* (Grand Rapids: Baker, 2008), p. 41.

as interpretation that takes up the insight of the precritical period can easily become a way of furthering what are actually modern concerns. That dynamic is characteristic of interpretation that focuses on the importance of peacemaking and nonviolence, concerns that take their agenda from modernity. This fact does not make them wrong, but we need to be rescued from reading our modern concerns into the agenda of earlier interpreters. The point applies also to the inclination to read a modern concern with nonviolence and peacemaking into Jesus' agenda.

PRAYER AND ETHICS

The problem with allegorical interpretation, then, is usually not what it says but what it fails to say. A Christian who undertakes allegorical interpretation is unlikely to make the text say something that disagrees with Christian faith, with biblical faith. The problem is that allegorical interpretation makes it possible to rework the text's meaning so that it says something that fits with the interpreter's understanding of what counts as Christian and biblical, and also to prevent the text from saying something that conflicts with that understanding.[19]

The most worrying aspect of allegorical interpretation of the Psalms is that it stops the Psalms having an ethical impact on us. The Psalms illustrate the way poetry can (a) evoke an atmosphere and an emotion, (b) entice people into its midst before they find out what role they are playing, (c) put readers into the shoes of other people in an emotional and not merely a rational way, (d) help readers identify themselves as perpetrators, (e) do so by sneaking up on readers rather than relating to them as if they were people taking part in a court of law or even as people listening to a story, (f) give readers a way of expressing their desire for redress, (g) give readers a way of seeking redress without actually taking action, (h) nevertheless give readers God's point of view on their lives, and (i) show readers a path from anguish to healing.[20]

The imprecatory psalms illustrate those insights particularly forcibly. I have argued that the imprecatory psalms enable us to take up our role as intercessors for the victims of oppression. It is a crucial role when we are in no

---

[19]Cf. James Barr, *Old and New in Interpretation* (New York: Harper, 1966), pp. 108-9.

[20]So Kathleen Scott Goldingay in a paper on the link between poetry and ethics in the Psalms, entitled "Fangs Dripping with Honey." The following paragraph also issues from insights in that paper, which appears together with the second half of this chapter under the title "The Sting in the Psalms" in *Theology* 114 (2014): 403-10 and 115 (2015): 3-9.

position to do anything about the oppression, but it is just as crucial when we *are* in a position to do something, because they remind us that what we do is not decisive. And I have argued that the imprecatory psalms have the capacity to scare the pants off us as oppressors and pull us to a change of life. Those nine points from (a) to (i) undergird these two. Their implication is that poetry makes a unique contribution to ethics because it performs moral correction on us as we perform it. The world of the Psalms is an ethical place, a place of truth. It defines the unfairness, instability and despair of the world we live in. As the words of the Psalms come out of our mouth, we are yoked to moral principles and concerns that come from beyond us. They are human words but they are human words that the people of God recognized as acceptable to God, as reflecting God's perspective. Because we read the Psalms out loud, we are involved in them. The verb *qārā'* is suggestive: when we read the Psalms, literally we call them, and in the process they call us. In taking them on our lips, we are pulled along by God's yoke, plowing a furrow of truth that we could not navigate alone but also that we cannot escape. During the singing of a psalm, God's justice thrives. Evildoers who seem to flourish are actually doomed. We can look around at a situation where God's justice is not thriving and say, "I want what I hear and see in the Psalms." And when we meet an enemy, we can threaten them with, "Have I got a psalm for you!"

Costly indeed is the loss of First Testament spirituality.

- 7 -

Memory and Israel's Faith, Hope and Life

Sometime in the first millennium A.D., the Torah, the Prophets and the Writings became in a Christian context the Old Testament.[1] During the second millennium, books such as Kings and Chronicles became histories. At the end of the second millennium they became narratives, and the Old Testament as a whole became the Hebrew Bible. These frameworks (Old Testament, histories, narratives, Hebrew Bible) sometimes facilitated but sometimes skewed the interpretation of the books. We have noted earlier in this volume that memory is of vital importance to spirituality and ethics, and that memory has become a topic of interest in a wide range of disciplines, including Jewish Studies, New Testament studies and Old Testament studies. One can thus look at the Torah, the Prophets and the Writings as the deposit of Israel's memory; indeed, given that memory is a category that explicitly appears in the First Testament, maybe it could help us get inside an aspect of its own way of thinking. While the Torah, the Prophets and the Writings do not begin with an instruction to remember, they begin with a huge exercise in memory, in Genesis–Kings. The scriptural position and order of Chronicles–Ezra–Nehemiah is less fixed,[2] but those narratives also imply an instruction to remember. Both sequences are exercises in memory,

---

[1] On the question when this title came into being, see the note at the end of the introduction to this volume.

[2] In some Hebrew manuscripts Chronicles opens and Ezra–Nehemiah closes the Writings; in others, the Writings close with Ezra–Nehemiah followed by Chronicles. In the Greek Bible and thus in the English Bible, these books follow Kings.

whose form results from the recycling of earlier memories. In studying them, we are concerned with the way the First Testament remembers and talks about memory, and with the way memory relates to Israel's faith, its hope and its ethics—in each case not Israel as it actually was, but Israel as the Torah, the Prophets and the Writings wish it to be or wish it had been.

MEMORY AND ISRAEL'S FAITH

While the Torah as a whole does not actually begin with explicit exhortation to remember, at its close Deuteronomy is the great book of such exhortation. "Remember the days of old, consider the years of generations long past, ask your father, and he will explain to you, your elders, and they will tell you" (Deut 32:7). "Take care for yourself and be very careful of yourself so you do not forget the things your eyes have seen, and so they do not turn aside from your mind all the days of your life. Make them known to your children and your grandchildren" (Deut 4:9). "Take care for yourself so that you do not forget Yahweh who got you out of the country of Egypt, out of a household of serfs" (Deut 6:12; see also, e.g., Deut 8:11; Ex 10:2; 13:3). Getting the Israelites out of Egypt constituted an assertion and reaffirmation of Yahweh's ownership of Israel, which puts the nation under double obligation to be committed to Yahweh and not to rebel. The point finds expression in the first of the Ten Commandments, since it was Yahweh who asserted ownership in this way (cf. Deut 8:19). It also finds expression in the second commandment, about making images, even of Yahweh, because the acts of Yahweh associated with the exodus and Sinai show that Yahweh is not a deity who can be imaged (Deut 4:23). Memory is vital to the fulfilling of those obligations.

Israel also needs to remember the long way Yahweh led it in the wilderness, to humble it and discover whether it would keep his commandments, and to remember its acts of rebellion during that time and their negative consequences (Deut 8:2; 9:7). There is thus something to be said for remembering one's shame (e.g., Ezek 16:63). Paradoxically, in the land the pressure of abundance, too, will mean Israel will need to cultivate memory (Deut 8:11-20). They must "master the trick of remembering privation in the midst of abundance"; it will be one of the reasons why they will need "a counterfactual memory" such as "keeps present to the mind a yesterday that conflicts with every today,"[3] and specifically to ensure that they live in the world without feeling at home in it. Because this memory, far from making you feel at home, denies you a home, it is greatly at risk. In Israel the Rekabites fulfill an important role in connection with maintaining this memory (see Jer 35).

Deuteronomy's "theory of individual, collective, and cultural memory" has made it possible to reckon that "the entire book is based on the deep fear of forgetting."[4] Memory is a struggle against forgetting.[5] Indeed Yosef Yerushalmi observes that in the Bible forgetting is always a terror.[6] Yet Yerushalmi thus contradicts something he said earlier (perhaps he had forgotten it) in noting that Israel is not commissioned to remember everything, only certain things.[7] Deuteronomy itself also urges the importance of forgetting. The First Testament incorporates many exhortations to forget, to put out of mind. Remembering involves forgetting.[8] Memory has to negotiate with forgetting, in order to remember and forget the right things.[9] While history in the sense of the events of the past incorporates everything that has happened, memory not only could not do so, but should not do so if it is to fulfill its function. Forgetting is the companion of remembering, in a good sense as well as a bad sense. There can be no such thing as an exhaustive narrative, and no such thing as an exhaustive memory. There has to be omission. Two contrary assertions are thus appropriate to the relationship between remembering and forgetting. Remembering excludes forgetting; remembering involves forgetting.[10]

You remember more if you forget some, if you focus. The Jerusalem court had an official called a *mazkîr* (1 Kings 4:3), whose title may suggest a recorder

---

[3]Jan Assmann, *Religion and Cultural Memory* (Stanford: Stanford University Press, 2006), p. 53.

[4]Ibid., p. 52.

[5]Paul Ricoeur, *Memory, History, Forgetting* (Chicago: University of Chicago, 2004), p. 413.

[6]Yosef Yerushalmi, *Zakhor: Jewish History and Jewish Memory* (reprinted New York: Schocken, 1989), pp. 108-9. Kerwin Lee Klein traces the beginning of the "scholarly boom" in memory studies to the original publication of *Zakhor* in 1982 ("On the Emergence of *Memory* in Historical Discourse," *Representations* 69 [2000]: 127-50 [127]).

[7]Yerushalmi, *Zakhor*, pp. 10-11.

[8]Jonathan Crewe, "Recalling Adamastor," summarizing Maurice Halbwachs (see his *On Collective Memory* [Chicago: University of Chicago, 1992]), in *Acts of Memory*, ed. Mieke Bal et al. (Hanover, NH: University Press of New England, 1999), pp. 75-86 (p. 75). Cf. James Fentress and Chris Wickham, *Social Memory* (Oxford: Blackwell, 1992), p. 39, referring to Mary Warnock, *Memory* (London: Faber, 1987).

[9]Ricoeur, *Memory, History, Forgetting*, p. 413.

[10]On the "dialectical tension" over remembering and forgetting, see John Barton, "Forgiveness and Memory in the Old Testament," in *Gott und Mensch*, ed. Markus Witte, Otto Kaiser festschrift (Berlin: De Gruyter, 2005), 1:987-95 (p. 994).

whose task included making sure that things were remembered. Some of these records would take the form of the annals that are referenced elsewhere. This understanding of the *mazkîr*'s role may rely too much on etymology,[11] but presumably *someone* had the task of keeping those annals. Yet ironically, the annals were only the place you might go for hard information about events, as opposed to the kind of story the Books of Kings told. The Books of Kings refer you to the annals for the mere hard facts as opposed to memories (1 Kings 14:19, 29). Israel didn't preserve the annals; it preserved the narratives,[12] which made the connection between past and present in which it was interested. So while memory preserves less than history, in another sense it incorporates more than history, by interpreting what it remembers, and also by the selectivity that focuses on things that seem especially important.

CONFLICTS OF MEMORY

Whereas other religions might have to be wary of ignoring an important deity, Israel has to forget some allegedly important deities. In this connection, the verb *shākaḥ* virtually means "repress."[13] Such forgetting is hard because the gods of everyday life who are to be renounced have been evidenced to people's senses.[14] Collective memory, or rather collective amnesia, "helped Israel forget about its own polytheistic past, and in turn it served to induce a collective amnesia about the other gods, namely, that many of these had been Israel's in the first place."[15] Thus archeology tells us about aspects of Israelite religion that its memory does not tell us of, because its official memory, preserved in the First Testament, did not wish them to be remembered. Kings and Chronicles tell a story that indicates what people should remember and how they should remember it, and also what they should forget.

One should not overstate the point—the memory of Israel's adherence to other gods is preserved in the text; it does not have to be excavated. The texts do not have to be read against the grain. They themselves tell the history of

---

[11] Cf. H. Eising, in *Theological Dictionary of the Old Testament*, ed. G. Johannes Botterweck et al. (Grand Rapids: Eerdmans, 1980), 4:64-82 (pp. 75-76).
[12] Yerushalmi, *Zakhor*, p. 15
[13] Assmann, *Religion and Cultural Memory*, p. 55.
[14] Ibid., p. 57.
[15] Mark S. Smith, *The Memoirs of God: History, Memory and the Experience of the Divine in Ancient Israel* (Minneapolis: Fortress, 2004), p. 5.

monotheism in Israel as a history of "memory, remembrance, forgetting, and the repressed, of trauma and guilt."[16] But they do such an effective job of commending what should be remembered that they succeed in getting readers not to notice the things that they report but do not commend. A further feature of the way in which Deuteronomy "frequently addresses . . . the problem of memory" is that it does so in connection with urging the importance of acknowledging Yahweh alone; "remembering YHWH is a difficult challenge."[17]

Memory is often contested. "Remind me," Yahweh challenges Israel, confrontationally (Is 43:26). The same prophecy also urges people to "remember" Abraham and Sarah (Is 51:1-2). Yet when they had encouraged themselves by the memory of Abraham at an earlier point, Ezekiel had warned them not to do so (Ezek 33:23-29).

> The memory of Abraham serves in varying measures to articulate Israelite identity, to motivate the remembering agent to take appropriate actions, to give solace, and to activate social, religious, or political ideals. These memories also serve to mask ambiguities and to create new fissures and oppositions where none were apparent previously. Some of these conditions of memory apply when God is the rememberer, others when humans are; the importance of remembering Abraham embraces both God and Israel. The implications of remembering Abraham are mutable.[18]

That comment leads into a further observation. Memory is capable of preserving ambiguity. The date and the social context of Genesis–Kings and of Chronicles–Ezra–Nehemiah in the form in which we have them, and of the earlier memories that they preserve, are matters of disagreement, and there is no sign that this disagreement will ever be resolved.[19] But the study of social memory recognizes that memories need to be interpreted on two levels. "Memories have their own specific grammars, and can (must) be analysed as narratives" even though "they also have functions, and can (must) be analysed in a

---

[16]Assmann, *Religion and Cultural Memory*, p. 51.

[17]Nathan MacDonald, *Deuteronomy and the Meaning of "Monotheism"* (Tübingen: Mohr, 2003), pp. 124, 149.

[18]Ronald Hendel, *Remembering Abraham* (Oxford: Oxford University Press, 2005), p. 31.

[19]It is possible to read the Pentateuch as the product of the selective memory that formed the Second Temple community (cf. Joseph Blenkinsopp, "Memory, Tradition and the Construction of the Past in Ancient Israel," *Biblical Theology Bulletin* 27 [1997]: 76–82 [80]). But this understanding explains only elements of the Pentateuch; and anyway, Chronicles and Ezra–Nehemiah are more certainly designed to fulfill this function for the Second Temple community.

functionalist manner, as guides . . . to social identity."[20] The documents that make up the Torah, the Prophets and the Writings, and the earlier works that lie behind them, originally functioned to shape memory in particular contexts to particular ends, but some communities thought they could also do so outside the contexts in which they emerged. One way of dealing with the aporia over determining the origin and context of works such as Genesis–Kings and Chronicles–Ezra–Nehemiah, then, is to focus on the text that we have, working with the way it has concealed the context out of which it emerged, rather than resisting this concealing (as it is appropriate to do in other forms of study). "From a theological perspective, the Bible is the revelation of what God selected to be remembered and forgotten of God's relationship to Israel and to the world" and of "God's own character and configuration."[21]

Memory and Ambiguity

Replacing history by memory doesn't solve the difficulties involved in asking historical questions, but it does provide another way of approaching them or of sidestepping them when they look as if they lead into a marsh. It provides a way of avoiding being hamstrung by the question in what sense the books are ideological, whether they serve the winners or the losers, the powerful or the weak. Like recalling Abraham, recalling the exodus can have many kinds of significance. It can aim to admonish and present moral demands, effect joy and gratitude, bring hope in distress, affirm Yahweh's actuality, and justify cultic and administrative enterprises. The description of exodus and covenant "presents not so much the tangled meanders of human memories but, rather, a variety of theological interpretations."[22] Biblical narrative "provides a picture of the past that bonds the community, provides the charter for its various ways of life and its visions of the future, and thus constructs and confirms a view of Israel's communal identity." In doing so, it "incorporates an endless variety of different voices."[23] It remembers things in ways that express their significance

---

[20]Fentress and Wickham, *Social Memory*, p. 88; cf. Ritva Williams, "Social Memory," *Biblical Theology Bulletin* 41 (2011): 189-200 (192).

[21]Smith, *The Memoirs of God*, p. 158.

[22]Teresa Staneck, "Exodus-Covenant," in *Performing Memory in Biblical Narrative and Beyond*, ed. Athalya Brenner and Frank H. Polak (Sheffield: Sheffield Phoenix, 2009), pp. 106-25 (pp. 113, 106-7).

[23]Frank H. Polak, "Negotiations, Social Drama and Voices of Memory in Some Samuel Tales," in Brenner and Polak, *Performing Memory*, pp. 46-71 (p. 46).

for the people who do the remembering. The plural "ways" is important. "Biblical 'history' is not just one memory . . . but a memory that is really a combination of collective memories. . . . The Bible is dialogical: it represents dominant, but also submerged voices, identities, and recollections."[24] For example, the First Testament often declares that it is impossible or inadvisable to see God, yet it also preserves a memory about Moses and his entourage seeing God (Ex 24:9-11).[25] It declares that God does not abandon his people, yet it also preserves a memory about God acknowledging that he had done so (Is 54:7). It declares that God tells Abraham to evict Hagar, yet it also preserves a memory about Hagar being the first person to name God (Gen 16:13).

At some points, then, Israel was happy to affirm conflicting memories, because they all contained truth. At other points it was unwilling to do so. It felt differently concerning that memory about seeing God from the way it felt about the memory of treating Yahweh as having a consort. Archeological discoveries suggest that Yahweh could be understood to have a consort, and that this understanding was not merely part of unofficial or private religion but part of public, official religion.[26] In Israel, the memory of the community's worshiping Yahweh's consort is construed differently by the people whose memory is reported in Jeremiah 44 and by the people who wrote that narrative. Memory is regularly contested. While the First Testament preserves reference to Israel's acknowledging other deities, male and female, it has eliminated this memory from its account of what counted as proper Israelite religion.

Michel Foucault argues that "since memory is actually a very important factor in struggle . . . , if one controls people's memory, one controls their dynamism. And one also controls their experience, their knowledge of previous struggles. . . . It is vital to have possession of this memory."[27] Yet how far is it possible to control people's memory? Memory can surely subvert the powers that seek control. In the short term, at least, the account of Israel's

---

[24]Philip R. Davies, "Story, Memory, Identity: Benjamin," in Brenner and Polak, *Performing Memory*, pp. 35-45 (p. 44).

[25]See Smith, *The Memoirs of God*, pp. 141-46.

[26]Cf. Mark S. Smith, "Remembering God," *Catholic Biblical Quarterly* 64 (2002): 631-51; Smith speaks of Israel's "conceptual amnesia about divinity" (p. 649).

[27]Michel Foucault, "Film and Popular Memory," in *Foucault Live* (New York: Semiotext[e], 1989), pp. 89-106 (p. 92).

story in the Books of Kings failed to determine how people would now relate to Yahweh and to other deities. Judah as a whole did not submit to the perspective commended by the books. "Although memory sustains hegemony, it also subverts it through its capacity to recollect and to restore the alternative discourses the dominant would simply bleach out and forget."[28] In the First Testament, there is a canonization from below against the monarchy (in Deuteronomy), a canonization from below against the hegemony of the imperial culture (in exilic writings) and a canonization from above by the authorization of the imperial authority (in Ezra).[29] Further, there can be an ambiguity within these embodiments of memory. The attitude taken to the Persian authorities in Ezra–Nehemiah is both positive and negative. Narrative memory is indeed capable of preserving ambiguity. Writing supports memory and creates a symbolic order that undergirds the state;[30] yet Isaiah and Jeremiah have their words written down, to subvert the state. Memory can preserve plurality, complexity and ambiguity.

Memory and Israel's Hope

According to Elie Wiesel, "remember" is the most frequent command in the Bible.[31] It's an exaggeration; my wife thought that "don't be afraid" was the most frequent command in the Bible. Then we realized that these two commands can be connected: one key to avoiding fear is to remember. Deuteronomy bids Israel not to be afraid of the Canaanites but to remember carefully what Yahweh did to Egypt (Deut 7:18; cf. Josh 1:13). In keeping with the complementary nature of remembering and forgetting, forgetting can also be a safeguard against fear. The promise that people will be able to forget their past shame is a key to avoiding fear (Is 54:4). Deuteronomy's "elaborate set of cultural memory techniques" to ensure that Yahweh's acts and the revelation of Yahweh's expectations "are handed down to future generations and are not forgotten" reinforce memory when the present offers it no support. They reinforce memory's "counterfactual" nature.[32]

---

[28]Richard Terdiman, *Present Past* (Ithaca, NY: Cornell University Press, 1993), p. 20.
[29]Assmann, *Religion and Cultural Memory*, p. 71.
[30]Ibid., p. 85.
[31]Elie Wiesel, "Hope, Despair and Memory," Nobel Peace Prize Lecture, December 11, 1986, http://www.nobelprize.org/nobel_prizes/peace/laureates/1986/wiesel-lecture.html.
[32]Assmann, *Religion and Cultural Memory*, pp. 55, 10-11, 16.

Memory encourages or discourages hope, depending on what you remember. According to Lamentations, after the fall of Jerusalem the city remembered its great past and remembered its more recent experience of distress, but it did not "remember" its future (Lam 1:7, 9; 3:19-20). In such contexts, human remembering is both painful and hopeful: "I shall remember God and complain. . . . I shall remember my song at night. . . . I shall cause Yahweh's deeds to be remembered; I shall remember your wonders of old" (Ps 77:3, 6, 11 [4, 7, 12]). Memory can help people cope with disaster or disappointment.

Given that the ability to influence if not to control social memory is associated with power and status, who gets to tell the story has important consequences. Social memory is malleable, vulnerable to manipulation, neglect and loss. The Psalms are an official version of how people are encouraged to pray, though that fact makes it the more striking that they incorporate much material that undercuts the power and authority of people in power, not least God. They thus embody or at least parallel what Foucault, again, calls "counter-memory," an individual or a small group's resistance to the official versions of the past as it affects the present.[33] The prayer in Isaiah 63:7–64:12 [11] begins, "I will cause Yahweh's acts of commitment to be remembered," but the intention is to face Yahweh with the tension between those past acts and the present neglect. The pressure of deprivation often issued in Israel's rebellions, and that pressure is a reality in Canaan. "Here we are concerned with a memory that finds no confirmation in the existing framework of the present, and, indeed, that even contradicts it."[34]

"Remember his covenant forever," the Asaphites thus urge in 1 Chronicles 16:15, in a hymn of praise that also appears in the Psalms. Neatly, however, the version in Psalm 105:8 declares that "*Yahweh has* remembered his covenant forever." It is the other side of the coin. We are to remember; God remembers. Israel is to remember Abraham (Is 51:2); God remembers Abraham or promises to do so (Ex 2:24; Lev 26:42). "He will not forget the covenant with your ancestors that he swore to them," Moses promises (Deut

---

[33]E.g., Michel Foucault, *Language, Counter-Memory, Practice* (Ithaca, NY: Cornell University Press, 1977).
[34]Assmann, *Religion and Cultural Memory*, p. 54.

4:31). As God urges us to remember, so we urge God to remember. On Sinai, Moses urges God to remember the ancestors and the oath he swore to them to multiply their descendants and give them a country of their own (Ex 32:13; cf. Deut 9:27), rather than remembering the people's sins of the past (Ps 79:8; cf. 25:7; Neh 1:8). Nehemiah even asks God to remember his good actions (Neh 5:19; 13:22). "The phrase 'God remembers' . . . appears to have its original context within the structure of the hymn," and the imperative "remember" characteristically appears in protest psalms;[35] the practice of remembering is at least as integral to thanksgiving psalms. The fall of Jerusalem was an occasion when Yahweh did not remember his footstool (Lam 2:1). Only near the end of Lamentations do people bid Yahweh remember what has happened to the city, but they also go on to ask there why he has utterly forgotten them (Lam 5:1, 20).

MEMORY, PAST AND PRESENT

A prayer for Jewish fast days recalls the many occasions when God has answered his people's prayers, and thus asks,

> May the One who answered Abraham our father on Mount Moriah,
> May the One who answered Sarah our mother at the door of the tent,
> May the One who answered our ancestors at the Sea of Reeds,
> May the One who answered Joshua at Gilgal,
> May the One who answered Deborah at Mount Tabor
> May the One who answered Samuel at Mizpah
> May the One who answered David and Solomon in Jerusalem
> May the One who answered Elijah on Mount Carmel
> May the One who answered Jonah in the insides of the fish
> May the One who answered Mordecai and Esther in Susa
> (and so on)

. . . may he "answer you and hearken to the sound of your cry this day."[36] The memories shape the hope and the prayers. It is in light of the way the Scriptures provide so much insight on God's involvement with his people and so much recollection of it, Yerushalmi comments, that after Josephus Jews did

---

[35]Brevard S. Childs, *Memory and Tradition in Israel* (London: SCM, 1962), pp. 41, 35.
[36]The motif goes back to the Mishnah (*Mo'ed Ta'anit* 2; about A.D. 200?) but it can be expanded in different ways (cf. Yerushalmi, *Zakhor*, p. 29).

not write historiography for centuries. Reading through Scripture each year in the lectionary meant that their ancestor Joseph did not get imprisoned and released only once in the long-gone past. It was a reality every year. Likewise people declare at Passover, "This *is* the bread of affliction": memory is not simply recollection but reactualization. Although the events happened once for all, they are experienced atemporally. While medieval Jews knew Babylon and Rome as the destroyers of the temple, neither Babylon nor Rome were historical realities for them, yet as they remembered the events, they experienced them. The refrain in a lament for Tisha be'Av speaks of when "I" experienced the fall of Jerusalem. Memory makes that process possible.[37] In the context of the Crusades, the story of the offering of Isaac resonated afresh. "While the horror remained vivid, it was no longer absurd, and grief, though profound, could be at least partly assuaged."[38] Michael V. Fox provides a parallel in describing his annual involvement in the reading of the story of Esther.

> Every year at Purim when I hear the Scroll read in the synagogue, I know that it is *true*, whatever the historical accuracy of its details. . . . Almost without an effort of imagination, I feel something of the anxiety that seized the Jews of Persia upon hearing of Haman's threat to their lives, and I join in their exhilaration at their deliverance. Except that I do not think "their," but "my."[39]

Fox goes on to describe some of the "antisemitic horrors" of the twentieth century that his family narrowly escaped. "I know the sense of precariousness that impelled Esther's author to insist on the inner powers of a vulnerable people but also—somewhat irrationally—on the certainty of their deliverance."[40] In remembering events in this way, Jews have been continuing to relate to them in the way Moses commends in his introduction to the Decalogue: Yahweh made the covenant at Horeb with Moses' hearers, not with their parents or ancestors (Deut 5:2-5).

---

[37]Yerushalmi, *Zakhor*, pp. 16, 22, 31, 34, 41-45.
[38]Ibid., p. 39.
[39]Michael V. Fox, *Character and Ideology in the Book of Esther*, 2nd ed. (Grand Rapids: Eerdmans, 2001), p. 11.
[40]Ibid., p. 12.

Memory After Judah's Downfall and
After Its Restoration

We have considered Genesis–Kings and Chronicles–Ezra–Nehemiah as two great scriptural middle narratives; as such, they are also the successive formulations of Israel's corporate memory. After the fall of Jerusalem, the community that had been overwhelmed by disaster looked to the past for understanding. However many editions of the Books of Kings there were, I assume that an important one was produced in this context, and their account of Israel's story addresses the Judahite community in order to encourage it to remember its story, and to remember it in a certain way. They seek to shape Judah's collective memory, the memory of the past that the authors wanted to mold people's attitudes in the present. The construction of memory they express is the means whereby the past might frame the present. They explain how the present emerged from the past and thus enable people to understand the present and begin to hope for the future. They illustrate the way social memory works, by continuously condensing, sorting, re-sorting, organizing and reorganizing the data it receives, to connect where we are now to where we have been in the past. It recalls events that have unified, animated, oriented or reoriented the community in fundamental ways, and presents these watershed moments as frameworks for evaluating and navigating through current circumstances.[41]

It might seem that remembering your past as a story of disobedience would be discouraging. The implication of the portrayal in Kings is the opposite. In inviting the community to face facts, it assumes that only when people have done so is there the possibility of facing the future and of having hope. God may grant them a future simply because of his mercy and not because they have faced facts, and indeed God seems to have done so (the epilogue to Kings in 2 Kings 25:27-30 points in this direction). But if they want to make any movement themselves toward having a future, remembering the past in a way that does justice to the facts is a place to start.

Chronicles–Ezra–Nehemiah does not reflect such a situation of disaster and tragedy. Chronicles knows more than Kings about the process

---

[41]Williams, "Social Memory," pp. 189-200.

whereby God manifested that mercy, as it shows by its own epilogue, and Ezra–Nehemiah can go on to remember the rebuilding of the temple and the work of Ezra and Nehemiah themselves. Yet the books do reflect a situation of disappointment and failure. The weeping in Ezra 3 is commonly read to reflect disappointment with the Second Temple as it is being built. Certainly the prayers in Ezra 9 and Nehemiah 9 express disappointment with the commitment of the Second Temple community, and with its continuing subjection to foreign kings, while Nehemiah is disappointed with the state of the city and with the division within the community.

The discouraging state of things encourages Chronicles to reframe the community's memory in a different way from the one in Kings, especially by remembering the way David set up the worship of the temple, in which the Judahites are privileged to take part. It has been assumed that the account of David in Chronicles is implicitly messianic: its emphasis on David implies the promise that God will reestablish David's throne. This scholarly assumption may issue from puzzlement about what other point the emphasis on David might have, but reflection on the significance of memory may facilitate the answering of this question. Remembering David, as Chronicles does, helps the community understand itself as a worshiping community.

Memory and History

Much of the account in Chronicles of David is imaginary, which points to another sense in which memory incorporates both less than history and more than history. It can forget; in addition, in offering an interpretation of events in light of its own day, it can embellish. The framework of memory thus helps us rethink the hoary question of the relationship between theology and history—not to resolve the question, but to approach it from another angle.

An interpretation of past events may both reflect and shape the way current events are perceived and lived with, so that it becomes a lens through which the community perceives reality and looks to the future. We may then call it the community's myth.[42] But *myth* can also suggest something that never hap-

---

[42]Natalia Bratova, "The Myth of St Petersburg in the Contemporary Russian Cinema. Balabanov's *Brother*," in *The Poetics of Memory in Post-Totalitarian Narration*, ed. Johanna Lindbladh (Lund: Lund University, 2008), pp. 121-25 (p. 125).

pened. We do talk about remembering something as having happened in a certain way when it did not, but then we are using the word *remember* in a Pickwickian fashion.[43] In theory, by its nature memory refers to things that did happen. Amos Funkenstein describes Ruth, Job, Jonah and Esther as historical novels, but then as reflexive literature.[44] While I can imagine that the author of Jonah knew he was writing a piece of fiction, even though he was writing about a real prophet, I do not think of Jonah as an exercise in memory. It seems less likely that the authors of Chronicles thought in a parallel way and more likely that the Books of Chronicles were written and received as a story that reminded people of who they were on the basis of reminding them of who they really had been. Fictionalized history functions similarly in our culture. Movies such as *Lincoln* and *Zero Dark Thirty* (about the killing of Osama bin Laden), for instance, seek to tell Americans something about themselves. The authors of such stories base them on fact, but use their imagination in order to get purchase in the present. Talk in terms of memory preserves the distinction between Chronicles and Jonah. Both sought to shape people's thinking and lives, but they did so on different bases.

Deuteronomy, while urging the importance of memory and implicitly claiming to be in continuity with the past, is in some ways expounding novel teaching, in the manner of Harold Bloom's bold rereading of texts.[45] But if Deuteronomy is a revisionist exercise in memory, it is surely claiming to be one that Moses or the author of the covenant code would recognize. Or if it was not making this claim, the authors of the Pentateuch were implying that they believed it to be so, though other Israelites would contest the point. Chronicles illustrates more clearly than Kings how the reformulating of memory can involve a fictionalizing of facts that is part of what makes possible the bridging of past and present. If one is trying to chart with accuracy the history of the events to which the story refers, the fictionalizing process is an unfortunate consequence of this bridging, but in terms of its own aim and what God may do through it, it is a positive aspect of the work.

So the fact that alleged past events have significance in the present might

[43]Mr. Pickwick in Charles Dickens's novel *The Pickwick Papers* used words with the opposite implications from what one would have assumed from their regular use.

[44]Amos Funkenstein, *Perceptions of Jewish History* (Berkeley: University of California, 1993), p. 57. Does he use *reflexive* in the sense of *reflective*?

[45]See *The Anxiety of Influence*, 2nd ed. (New York: Oxford University Press, 1997).

mean that they were invented to that end. Yet it is also the present significance of real past events that causes them to be remembered. Present relevance encourages both false memory and true memory.[46] Encouraging people to remember David doing things he did not do may involve the assumption that there was enough of a link between his historical acts and the worship of the Second Temple to justify this reformulating of his memory. Barry Schwartz has reflected on the memory of Abraham Lincoln in a way that provides a parallel.[47] In the 1960s, he argues, Lincoln's support was invoked for the granting of civil rights to African Americans, yet Lincoln's own support for the abolition of slavery had not extended this far. Yet there is some validity in the claim that in a twentieth-century context the granting of civil rights coheres with Lincoln's commitment to abolition. It is hard to imagine a 1960s Lincoln opposing civil rights.

So memory bridges past and present in a way that may falsify history but may also thereby be true to history. One cannot prove the point about Lincoln, or the point in Chronicles about David. All one can say is that the Second Temple community was sufficiently persuaded by the memory of Chronicles to incorporate it into its Scriptures. "Considering Lincoln's image as a mere projection of present problems is as wrong as taking it as a literal account of his life and character."[48] Memory selects from the real Lincoln and then projects forward to reject later convictions or ideals. Likewise it is mistaken to treat the First Testament narratives either as pure fact or as pure fiction. Minimalism emphasizes how the past is shaped by the present; maximalism works on the hypothesis that the present is shaped by the past. I guess that both minimalists and maximalists would grant that past and present are mutually influential.

In her study of the memory of the exodus, Teresa Staneck has commented that "some actual experiences hide concealed beyond those descriptions; however, it is impossible to recognise what exactly had happened." I acknowledge the truth in that statement. "From the perspective of sacred texts," she goes on, "the reality of events behind the narratives is irrelevant."[49] That

---

[46]Cf. Rafael Rodriguez, *Structuring Early Christian Memory* (New York: T & T Clark, 2010), pp. 53-54.

[47]Barry Schwartz, *Abraham Lincoln and the Forge of National Memory* (Chicago: University of Chicago Press, 2000).

[48]Ibid., p. 6.

[49]Staneck, "Exodus-Covenant," pp. 106-7.

second statement seems implausible. "The truthful status of memory . . . will later have to be confronted with the truth claims of history."[50] The having-happened-ness of the exodus surely mattered to the authors and readers of these sacred texts, and it is a stretch to imagine that the story of the exodus issued simply from the reworking of memories concerning an escape from quasi-Egyptian rule within Canaan, though one cannot rule out the possibility that such an actual event had enough significance to carry the theological freight of the way the story came to be told.

MEMORY AND ISRAEL'S ETHICS

As well as establishing who we are, cultural memory points toward what we should be and do; "the human animal . . . has been given memory so that it is capable of keeping a promise and undertaking responsibilities. Man needs a memory in order to live in a community."[51] Thus

> as a model *of* society, collective memory reflects past events in terms of needs, interest, fears, and aspirations of the present. As a model *for* society, collective memory performs two functions: it embodies a *template* that organizes and animates behavior and a *frame* with which people locate and find meaning for their present experience. Collective memory affects social reality by *reflecting, shaping, and framing* it.[52]

In the First Testament, one importance of remembering the exodus was its ethical implications. When Deuteronomy reworks the Sabbath command, it both underscores the aim that your servants should be able to rest in the same way as you, and replaces the reference to creation in the Exodus version by an exhortation to remember that you were a serf in Egypt and that Yahweh acted to bring you out from there (Deut 5:15). The challenge to "remember that you were a serf in Egypt" recurs in connection with the requirement that you should provide your servant with flocks, grain and wine when you free him at the end of his six-year term, that you should incorporate your servants in the observance of Sukkot, and that you should not

---

[50]Ricoeur, *Memory, History, Forgetting,* p. 4.
[51]Assmann, *Religion and Cultural Memory,* pp. 38, 53, summarizing Friedrich Nietzsche, *The Genealogy of Morals* (New York: Modern Library [no date]), pp. 40-47.
[52]Schwartz, *Abraham Lincoln and the Forge of National Memory,* p. 18. Cf. Rodriguez, *Structuring Early Christian Memory,* p. 54.

take legal advantage of alien, orphan and widow but should leave gleanings for them (Deut 15:12-15; 16:12; 24:17-22).[53]

The exhortation to remember occurs once more in Deuteronomy in a quite different connection. Israel is to remember Amalek's attacking it on the way from Egypt when people were exhausted, and its cutting down stragglers and thus showing no reverence for God. Israel is to blot out Amalek's memory from under the heavens, and not to forget to do so (Deut 25:17-19). Deuteronomy has again developed the Exodus version of the story; there it seems that Amalek's attack is simply unprovoked and Yahweh commissions the writing of a document to keep alive the memory of Yahweh's oath to blot out Amalek's memory. It is not explicit there that *Israel* is to remember; Exodus is reminding Israel of a promise concerning what Yahweh will do.

Deuteronomy's exhortation contrasts with a conviction implied elsewhere in the First Testament that one should be prepared to forgive and forget wrongdoing. Shimei urges David, "May my lord not count waywardness to me or remember how your servant went astray on the day my lord the king left Jerusalem," and David agrees, though on his deathbed he points out to Solomon that his son is not bound by his father's oath (2 Sam 19:19 [20]; 1 Kings 2:9). The Joseph story does not use the words *remember* or *forget*, but Joseph shows himself willing not to remember his brothers' wrongdoing.

Forgive and Forget?

The Amalek exhortation about memory has been an embarrassment to Jews and Christians for two thousand years.[54] Can it have any positive significance, make us think as well as provoke our indignation? Christians have sometimes identified other Christian groups as new embodiments of Amalek that should therefore be annihilated, but the First Testament does not suggest that Israel might or did look at adversaries other than Amalek in this way. The nearest is the identification of Haman in Esther as an Agagite; there is then also the irony that the Jewish people end up behaving

---

[53]The earlier exhortation to "remember the day of your departure from the country of Egypt" (Deut 16:3) by observing the flatbread festival does not incorporate reference to *'abādîm* or to the experience of being an *'ebed*.

[54]On the history of Jewish interpretation, see Avi Sagi, "The Punishment of Amalek in Jewish Tradition," *Harvard Theological Review* 87 (1994): 323-46. For examples of Christian appropriation of the texts, see Philip Jenkins, *Laying Down the Sword* (New York: HarperOne, 2011).

the same way as Haman in the story.[55] One should have some sympathy with Jewish identification of Nazi Germany as an embodiment of Amalek, and the question of remembering and forgetting the Holocaust is a lively one. Yerushalmi comments that the problem about memory is how much to remember and how much to forget, and asks whether the antonym of forgetting is not remembering but justice.[56] Forgetting can be ideological, like the European memory of the mid-twentieth century; the ambiguity of forgetting extends to the question of the obligation to forgive and the relationship of forgetting and forgiving.[57]

Perhaps the difference between the attitude of Joseph to his brothers and that of Moses to Amalek, and the difference between David's attitude to Shimei when he is returning to Jerusalem and when he is on his deathbed, relates to the difference between the attitude we may properly take individually to people who have wronged us and the attitude that a society may properly take to wrongdoing. Individuals turn the other cheek; societies punish the striker. When wrong is done, it throws the world out of kilter, and action taken against wrong reaffirms what is right.

Deuteronomy bases its argument for remembering Amalek on its having been the strong attacking the weak. Social memory can be presented as a realm of resistance against the public, dominant version of memory that is known as "history." If traditional history was a discourse about the past produced by the victors and privileging those who had generated written evidence, memory might be seen as the repository of knowledge of "people without history," or traumatized communities for whom remembering is an "act of faith."[58] One of our difficulties with the Amalek story as Western people is that we are Amalek. It's not in our interest for Amalek to be remembered in the way Deuteronomy encourages.

The trouble is that, in addition, "collective memory is particularly susceptible to politicized forms of remembering." Remembering the Battle of

---

[55]Cf. Stan Goldman, "Narrative and Ethical Ironies in Esther," *Journal for the Study of the Old Testament* 47 (1990): 15-31.

[56]Yerushalmi, *Zakhor*, pp. 114, 117.

[57]Ricoeur, *Memory, History, Forgetting*, pp. 412, 448.

[58]"Memory: Concepts and Theory," Research Institute for History, Leiden University, accessed July 16, 2014, www.hum.leiden.edu/history/talesoftherevolt/approach/approach-1.html, with references to scholars such as Yerushalmi.

Kosovo in 1389 and the Battle of the Boyne in 1690, as well as the fall of Masada and Auschwitz, has fueled conflicts.[59] Many conflicts persist because we cannot forget the past. Ernest Renan declared that "forgetting, I would even go so far as to say historical error, is a crucial factor in the creation of a nation."[60] Memory both stabilizes and destabilizes.[61] Nietzsche and Freud correlate memory with guilt and conscience. It's "the wound that does not cease to hurt."[62] Ideally, the responsibility to remember lies upon third parties, to remember on behalf of both the victims and the perpetrators. We have noted in chapter six that it is their responsibility to pray the protest psalms on behalf of both victims and perpetrators. If the perpetrators and the third parties don't forget, the victims can afford to do so and should do so, though they would be unwise to assume that this remembering will always persist, or will persist as long as it needs to (which is perhaps forever) to inhibit other perpetrators from repeating the same wrong.

By means of its festivals and other observances, but also by means of its Scriptures, Israel "constructs itself as a community of learning and remembering."[63] The First Testament thus sees remembering and forgetting as deliberate purposeful acts. It perhaps does not imply that they are always deliberate acts, and I'm not sure whether it is so. I suspect that some of my memories are random, but many are significant and in that sense deliberate. Perhaps some things that Israel remembers are random, but Israel certainly remembers things because they seem important and illuminating. They shape its faith, its hope, and its life—or at least, they are meant to do so. We are unwise not to join in the remembering that it has passed on to us.

---

[59] Assmann, *Religion and Cultural Memory*, p. 7.
[60] "What Is a Nation?" in *Nation and Narration*, ed. Homi K. Bhabha (New York: Routledge, 1990), pp. 8-22 (p. 11); cf. Hendel, *Remembering Abraham*, p. x.
[61] Cf. Terdiman, *Present Past*, pp. vii-viii.
[62] Assmann, *Religion and Cultural Memory*, p. 96.
[63] Ibid., p. 19.

8

Moses (and Jesus and Paul) for
Your Hardness of Hearts

Near the beginning of the Sermon on the Mount, Jesus notes that the people of old were told (for instance) not to murder or commit adultery, and to love their neighbors but hate their enemies; "I tell you," he says, that we should avoid the inner attitude that finds expression in murder or adultery, and should love our enemies (Mt 5:21-48). Western Christians often take his words as an indication that the New Testament's ethical ideals are higher than the First Testament's. If they are, how can the biblical material as a whole be a resource for ethics?

Several considerations suggest that this Western inference from Jesus' words is mistaken. First, the importance of inner attitude as well as outward act already features in the First Testament. Job's account of his life in Job 31 is a systematic exposition of this awareness, not least in connection with areas that appear in the Sermon on the Mount such as sex and murderous thinking. Joseph embodies the Sermon on the Mount in his forgiveness of his brothers, who have behaved toward him as enemies; turning the other cheek was not a new idea in the New Testament. Second, there is no First Testament exhortation to hate one's enemies. Indeed, Jesus himself is the only person in Scripture to tell anyone to hate anyone else. For that matter, there is no exhortation to hate one's enemies in any contemporary Jewish writings that we know. Jesus' reference to an encouragement to hate one's enemies is thus a puzzle. Third, the context in which Leviticus urges people to love their neighbor indicates that the neighbor whom they are to love is the neighbor who is their enemy, the person whom they might rebuke for doing wrong or from whom they might seek redress or against whom they might bear a grudge (Lev 19:17-18). Leviticus's own point, then, is that loving one's neighbor implies loving one's enemy (actually, people hardly need to be exhorted to love the neighbors with whom they get on).

The Torah does not refer to loving foreigners who are your enemies, though in effect the book of Jonah does, and Paul backs up his exhortation about relating positively to enemies with a quotation from Proverbs (Rom 12:9-21). The Torah itself does exhort Israelites to love the foreigner, using exactly the same expression that it uses for loving your neighbor (Lev 19:34). It is not the case, then, that "the Law limits the obligation of love to the neighbor (i.e., the fellow-Israelite)."[1] On the other hand, the New Testament is markedly inclined to focus the obligation of love on other members of the people of God (Jn 13:34; 1 Jn 3:11-24).

Fulfillment and Love

In his exhortation to love one's enemy Jesus is bringing out the Torah's own implications, not setting forth expectations that contrast with the Torah's. This aspect of his teaching thus fits the context in Matthew 5, whereas the common Western view fits ill with that context. In the introduction to the paragraphs in question Jesus declares that he has come to fulfill (*plēroō*) the Torah and the Prophets, not to annul them (Mt 5:17-20). He has already been doing something along these lines in the Blessings that precede that declaration. These Blessings are a profound, challenging and encouraging proclamation about spirituality, and in part they are so because they are fulfilling the Torah and the Prophets. Most of their raw materials come from Isaiah and the Psalms, though one of the most striking of the Blessings resonates with the Torah: whereas Jesus' blessing on peacemakers could seem to contrast with the Torah and the Prophets, it does evoke the way Israel does its best to negotiate a friendly passage through Edomite territory on its way to the Promised Land; when Israel receives a militaristic response, it withdraws in order to go another way (Num 20:14-21). Being peacemakers rather than war makers was not a new idea in the New Testament.

---

[1]Against Richard B. Hays, *The Moral Vision of the New Testament* (San Francisco: Harper, 1996), p. 96.

In introducing the question of the First Testament's ethics in chapter one, we noted that the notion of fulfillment is ambiguous. Fulfilling the Torah might simply mean obeying it (cf. Rom 8:4; 13:8). Yet even contexts that imply this meaning also suggest the connotation of filling up or filling out. This understanding makes sense in Matthew 5. In his teaching Jesus is bringing out the meaning of the Torah and the Prophets. Leviticus 19:18 implies loving one's enemy; Jesus makes the implication explicit. To anyone who knew the Scriptures, there was nothing revolutionary or shocking in his expectation that one should love one's enemies, though some people would no doubt find it offensive as they do today. In thus "fulfilling" the Torah, Jesus speaks as a prophet. He is acting in the same way as Micah when Micah opens up the question about what the good behavior that Yahweh looks for is, and answers that it involves implementing good judgment, giving yourself to commitment and being reticent in how you walk with your God (Mic 6:8). It sums up concerns of the Torah. Micah, too, is fulfilling the Torah. Prophets such as Isaiah and Amos condemn Israel's prayer and worship because they are unaccompanied by faithful relations within the community, and Leviticus carries the same implication, so they, too, are fulfilling the Torah.

Of course the attitude to enemies in the Torah, the Prophets and the Writings is more complex than the example of Joseph or the passage about Israel and Edom or the exhortation in Leviticus 19 might suggest. While there is love of enemies in the First Testament, there is also hatred of enemies and killing of enemies. Ironically, the Israelites' attacks on the Canaanites, which offend modern Westerners, are arguably not an example of hatred of enemies. The Canaanites were not Israel's enemies, and the account of Israel's attitude to the Canaanites does not refer to hating them. Israel was to attack them in an unprovoked way even though they were not their enemies, because God viewed them as his own enemies. Conversely, in the New Testament, too, there is hatred of enemies, such as the attitude Paul expresses in 2 Thessalonians 1.

Jesus' talk of fulfillment and his subsequent examples, then, point to one aspect of what is involved in interpreting the ethical implications of the biblical material. There are imperatives, and there are ways in which their implications need to be spelled out. Jesus makes a related point in responding to the classic Jewish question about the most important command in the Torah. His answer combines commands about love for God (Deut 6:5) and love for one's neighbor (Lev 19:18); he adds that the entirety of the Torah and the Prophets hangs on these two imperatives (Mt 22:34-40). With regard to the second of these commands, it follows that if you love your neighbor, you will fulfill the Torah (Gal 5:14). Jesus thus offers an alternative to the postmodern instinct to ask whose interest is served by commands in the Torah and elsewhere. The interpretive question he suggests is rather, how does any given command express love for God or love for one's neighbor?[2] He is not inviting people to make this question the "filter" by means of which they evaluate the Torah,[3] but the clue to seeing the Torah's own concerns. The implications are not so different when he sums up the Torah and the Prophets as "treat others the way you would have them treat you" (Mt 7:12). Our interest and the interest of the other might thus be brought together.

IDEAL AND CONDESCENSION

Alongside his words about fulfillment and about the twofold principle that underlies the entire Torah, a third comment by Jesus on the interpretation of the Torah offers a further related insight that stands closer to that postmodern instinct. It is the comment from which I take my chapter title. He is again responding to a question, concerning divorce. He rules out the idea that a man may initiate a divorce, because it does not fit Genesis 1–2. How then does he understand the regulation about giving a woman a divorce certificate (Deut 24:1)? "It was because of your stubbornness that Moses permitted you to divorce your wives, but from the beginning it was not like this" (Mt 19:1-12).

As is the case with his spelling out the implications of the Torah in Matthew 5 and Matthew 22, he is not here introducing an idea of his own. Deuteronomy itself is fond of describing Israel as stubborn (e.g., Deut 9:6, 13; 10:16). So he takes a critical stance in relation to the Torah, but this stance involves not introducing a new and higher standard than that of the Torah

---

[2]Philip Jenson posits a suggestive background to this understanding within Deuteronomy itself, whose rules represent three levels: (1) "The command," as Deut 6:1 puts it, the Shema; (2) "The ten words" (Deut 4:13); and (3) "The laws and decisions" (Deut 4:14). See Jenson, "Snakes and Ladders," in *Ethical and Unethical in the Old Testament*, ed. Katharine Dell (New York: T & T Clark, 2010), pp. 187-207, following Eugene H. Merrill, e.g., *Everlasting Dominion* (Nashville: Broadman, 2006), p. 164: "The Shema is to the Decalogue what the Decalogue is to the whole covenant text, especially in its Deuteronomic rendition."

[3]Against Hays, *The Moral Vision of the New Testament*, p. 101.

but analyzing the diversity of levels within the Torah itself. The regulation about divorce certificates stands in tension with Genesis, because it makes allowance for human stubbornness, but in keeping with Jesus' other comment, the regulation is also an expression of love, because it gives a woman some means of establishing her status; she cannot simply be thrown out by a husband who is tired with her.

There are further areas where the Torah implies a distinction between how things were from the beginning and how they are when one is being realistic about life in a stubborn world. The idea that husbands exercise authority over wives is the most explicit (Gen 3:16). The idea that a man might have more than one wife or that one human being might be the servant or slave of another are further implicit examples. Another tension within the Torah relates to the killing and eating of animals. Genesis 1 (from the Priestly narrative) states the ideal; humanity is to be vegetarian. Genesis 9 (also from the Priestly narrative) makes a concession in light of the human waywardness that succeeding chapters of Genesis have described. Leviticus 17 (from the Holiness Code) tightens the concession in requiring draining of the blood and killing the animal at the sanctuary. It thus takes one step back toward the ideal in its respect for animal life, in its assumption that shedding an animal's blood is wrong and in its concern for worship of Yahweh alone (as it takes a step backward toward the ideal in its Jubilee teaching). On the other hand, Leviticus itself does require much slaughter; it does not attempt to implement the vegetarian ideal. Deuteronomy 12 allows for killing animals away from the sanctuary and thus extends the concession. Historically Deuteronomy preceded the Holiness Code, but in the compiling of the Torah (by the authors of the Holiness Code?) Deuteronomy was allowed to stand at the end of the Torah and to have the last word.[4]

In his comment about fulfilling the Torah, Jesus challenges his disciples to show a righteousness exceeding that of the Pharisees and scholars. The discussion of divorce suggests what might be involved, namely, that one does not take advantage of regulations in the Torah that make it possible to evade the Torah's highest demands. The problem of "whose interest is being served" is not a problem within the text but a problem within interpreters. The text needs to be interpreted not in my own interests but as an expression

---

[4]So Joachim Schaper in a paper on "Ritual, Monotheism and the Place of Leviticus in the Pentateuch," given to the Society for Old Testament Study in Bangor, Wales, July 2013.

of love. Augustine's principle that the test of interpretation is whether it tends to build up the twofold love of God and neighbor[5] is not merely a principle for the application of the text but a principle for its exegesis that corresponds to Jesus' point about the Torah and the Prophets.

The disciples are horrified that they should have to forgo the right to divorce; they do not wish to aim at a higher righteousness than other people. Jesus then makes clear that he is not rigorous in the stance he takes; he recognizes that not everyone can accept it. Indeed, he himself does not seek to implement a standard that matches how things were at the beginning, in his approach to the position of men and women among his disciples. While there are positive aspects to his attitude to women, he includes no women among his twelve disciples, and the Gospels do not describe his calling any women to follow him. He does not take the egalitarian approach that is implicit in Genesis 1–2.

Jesus' attitude to the material in the Torah concerning divorce thus suggests a way of handling some troubling data within the New Testament. The "household codes" point to areas of life where the New Testament has lower standards than the First Testament. There is no expectation in the First Testament that wives should be silent when people gather for worship (1 Cor 14:34), and only the New Testament says that wives should obey their husbands (1 Pet 3:1). In regard to relations between the sexes, the New Testament arguably represents "an impoverishment of traditions."[6] This is not to say that it is not authoritative Scripture; there was apparently reason for allowing such exhortations to have a place in the New Testament. They illustrate the way the New Testament, like the First Testament, makes allowance for the hardness of human hearts. What such data in the New Testament do suggest is that we should not assume that the teaching of the First Testament is outdated by that of the New. Both Testaments are resources for the community's understanding of God's expectations.

THE CASE OF SLAVERY

I assume that the same principle underlies the New Testament's acceptance of slavery. People who supported slavery in the United States were easily able to

---

[5]*On Christian Doctrine* 1.36.
[6]Margaret Davies, "Work and Slavery in the New Testament," in *The Bible in Ethics*, ed. John W. Rogerson et al. (Sheffield: Sheffield Academic Press, 1995), pp. 315-47 (p. 347).

quote the New Testament to substantiate their case. Jesus and the New Testament writers refer many times to slaves and slave owners and never raise any questions about slavery. Indeed, the New Testament frequently urges slaves to obey their masters (1 Tim 6:1-2; Tit 2:9-10; 1 Pet 2:18-25). Paul does note that slaves and free are one in Christ Jesus (Gal 3:28), but the same is true of male and female, so the statement carries no implications regarding the abolition of the difference. In keeping with his comment about all being one in Christ Jesus, Paul urges Philemon to accept back his runaway slave Onesimus "no longer as a slave but more than a slave, a beloved brother" (Philem 16). The exhortation has been used to support their case both by abolitionists and by defenders of slavery. Perhaps Paul's ambiguity tests Philemon and indicates the same combination of attitudes as Jesus: releasing Onesimus would be great, but Paul is not insisting on it. While Ephesians 6:9 exhorts slave owners not to ill-treat their slaves, neither letter urges masters to free slaves after seven years of service in keeping with the Torah. Indeed, 1 Corinthians 7:17-24 includes slaves among the people who are urged to be content to stay as they are unless they happen to get an opportunity to find their freedom.

The argument in 1 Corinthians and in Philemon does introduce a new factor into the New Testament's exhortations concerning slavery, as does Ephesians 5–6 concerning marriage.[7] There, the expectation concerning a wife's submission to her husband is transformed as a result of the redefining of the husband's obligation. His job is to let himself be crucified on her behalf; her job is to submit to his doing so. Yet such reinterpretation of the expectations in the household codes is not a consistent feature of the way the New Testament reworks the household codes, and one can see that simply making Jesus' acceptance of ill-treatment a model for slaves (1 Pet 2:18-25) is potentially an oppressive move.

The place of slavery in the Roman Empire and its role in the way households worked may make it difficult to imagine what the abolition of slavery would look like or how it might be achieved. Yet the difference over against the situation in Israel is more one of degree than of kind. Even when one makes allowance for the kind of reinterpretation that appears in Ephesians and Philemon, it remains troublesome that the New Testament raises no

---

[7]See, e.g., Oliver O'Donovan, *The Desire of Nations* (Cambridge: Cambridge University Press, 1996), pp. 183-86; N. T. Wright, *Paul and the Faithfulness of God* (London: SPCK, 2013), pp. 3-22.

questions about the institution. It is all the more problematic given that the slavery of New Testament times is a much more oppressive institution than the short-term indentured labor caused by debt that is accepted by the Torah. The First Testament is mostly talking about something more like being a servant than being a slave. Indeed, such servitude commonly lasts only for a limited period and it's quite like being an employee—the ideal being that you work in the family business rather than work for someone else. New Testament slavery more commonly involves people becoming the property of other people and being subject to their absolute power. It is New Testament–like slavery that Britain eventually encouraged and America accepted. People found it easy to oppose the abolition of slavery on the basis of texts from Paul, while it is First Testament texts that give most support to abolition.

Augustine, again, saw sin as the prime cause of slavery. He notes that the word *slave* does not occur until Noah uses it. It's a name introduced by sin not by nature, he therefore comments.[8] In other words, "from the beginning it was not like this." Augustine's stance contrasts with that of Aristotle, who justified slavery on the basis of the conviction that there were natural differences between people born to be free and to rule, and people who did not have the gifts necessary to running their own lives, who needed to be subject to someone else.[9] While Thomas Aquinas's view was somewhere in between Aristotle and Augustine, he does note that Genesis 1 gives human beings dominion over the animate world but not over one another.[10]

It is in this connection that Margaret Davies comments on the contrast between the Testaments. The First Testament has two approaches to social ethics. On one hand, it legislates for the social order, attempting to place limits on the oppression of the weak by the powerful. On the other, it lays moral obligations before people, attempting to get them to be generous and considerate to the needy. In contrast, the New Testament writings "provide nothing like the breadth of vision in social affairs to be found in the Jewish scriptures." Further, "there is nothing in the New Testament to compare with Philo's description of Essene belief and practice: 'They denounce the owners of slaves, not merely for outraging the law of equality, but also for their im-

---

[8]*City of God* 19.15.
[9]See *Politics* 1.3-6.
[10]*Summa theologica* Supplement, Question 52, Article 1.

piety in annulling the statute of nature, who like a mother has borne and reared all alike as genuine brothers."' Thus "a comparison with Deuteronomy and Leviticus shows that the New Testament represents an impoverishment of traditions, an impoverishment which allowed gross injustice to flourish in Christian countries through the centuries."[11]

Jesus, then, suggests three hermeneutical clues for our interpretation of injunctions in the First Testament, clues we may apply to the New Testament, too. One is that it may involve bringing out the inherent implications of some injunction. Another is that it may involve asking how an injunction may be an expression of love for God or for one's neighbor. A third is that it may involve asking where an injunction stands on the axis that runs between God's creation will and God's making allowance for human stubbornness. Jesus does not suggest that he offers a more advanced understanding of ethics than the one in the Scriptures.

THE QUESTION ABOUT METHOD

Thus there is no "problem" about the relationship of the Testaments in connection with the level of their ethics. The tricky question regarding method in connection with biblical ethics is rather as follows. My inclination as a white Englishman is to come to the Bible with liberal Western values. These include beliefs such as the following: that individuals should be able to make their own decisions about what they do, rather than being forced to do what someone else says; that people should be able to appoint their own governments; that nations should not be subject to rule by other nations; that individuals should have the freedom to decide who to marry and should have the same opportunity for education and work whatever their sex or race; that we should abjure violence; that we should look after the world rather than despoil it; that individuals should have autonomy over their bodies, rather than being liable to torture, assault or abuse; that they should be free to worship as they wish, to act as they wish and to speak as they wish, as long as they do not harm other people in doing so. We could argue about some elements in that list or about their precise formulation or about whether other items should be added, but the general picture will do.

---

[11]Margaret Davies, "Work and Slavery in the New Testament," pp. 321, 342, 347.

David Clines observes that he evaluates the Torah in light of a similar set of standards, "the ethical standards . . . of a liberal Western conscience, affirming of personal dignity, individual and collective freedom and self-determination, and opposed to violence and discrimination, and so on."[12] He thus articulates a truth that is common though not commonly recognized or acknowledged. He is well aware that these standards are the values of our particular culture. We are inclined to think they are universal norms; as the American Declaration of Independence puts it, "We hold these truths to be self-evident." Yet the very formulation of the convictions in that declaration shows it to be affected by the culture in which it was formulated, and a consideration of values from other contexts confirms the point. The core African principles of Kwanzaa, for instance, are unity, self-determination, collective work and responsibility, cooperative economics, purpose, creativity, and faith. Asian values include a belief in consensus rather than confrontation, respect for authority and commitment to the well-being of the community over against that of individuals.

Readers of the Bible who are committed to accepting its authority are inclined simply to assume that their values and the Bible's values must be the same and thus to look for ways of conforming the two. Attitudes to violence are an example. In the present world,

> no documentation is really necessary to prove that violence is a societal scourge of monumental proportions and that it is escalating at a terrifying pace domestically, locally, nationally, and globally. And no one seems to have any idea how to stem the increase except to mobilize more and more "good" violence by arming more people, building more prisons, and declaring more wars, to combat the "bad" violence.[13]

Western readers expect to find their abjuring of violence in the Bible, and they do so by means of a selective reading of aspects of Jesus' teaching and of the significance of his life, and by means of an evaluative reading of other parts of the Bible on its basis. Readers who are more comfortable with a suspicious reading operate in a different way. Feminist interpretation, postcolonial interpretation, ecological interpretation and disability interpre-

---

[12]David Clines, "Does the Pentateuch Exist?" www.academia.edu/3859631, accessed February 4, 2014.
[13]Sandra M. Schneiders, "The Lamb of God and the Forgiveness of Sin(s) in the Fourth Gospel," *Catholic Biblical Quarterly* 73 (2011): 1-29 (2).

tation have some commonality of approach. Their starting point enables them to see ways in which the Bible has been misinterpreted and ways in which its implications have been missed; it can thus be harnessed to resource their perspective. Their starting point also provides them with a basis for critiquing the Bible. The starting point is an absolute; the approach to interpretation systematically rules out the possibility of self-critique. The starting point, the perspective they bring to the text, is the absolute.

We have noted that the problem with allegorical interpretation is that it can rework the text's meaning to make it say something that fits with the interpreter's understanding of what counts as Christian and biblical, and also prevent it from saying something that conflicts with that understanding. The difficulty with allegorical interpretation is not that it fails to be open to learning from its texts but that it learns only within the framework of its presuppositions.[14] The irony is that critical interpretation has the same problem.

The difficulty these considerations raise for interpretation is as follows. The diversity within the Scriptures means one can find material to support almost any position that one wishes to maintain. And the fact that both Testaments combine God's ideal vision with allowance for human stubbornness provides us with a golden key to using the Bible to support what we approve of (that's God's ideal) and to undermine what we don't approve of (that's material making allowance for human stubbornness). Yet whatever set of values we presuppose, we would surely be wise to assume that it should be treated as not final; we are likely to be wrong at some points. An awareness of another culture's values gives us something to think against in this connection, and at the very least, the Bible has the capacity to fulfill that function. In this connection readers (like me) who are predisposed to assume that the Bible gets things right will be wise to start from the assumption that there are likely to be differences between our values and the Bible's rather than the assumption that they are the same, and thus to look for the differences that will critique us. At the very least, we will be wise to seek to stay in ongoing dialogue with the parts of the Bible that we don't like. And if reading the Bible issues only in providing us with material that reinforces what we already think, our reading is very likely ideological.

---

[14]See the section on "Prayer and Ethics" in chapter six, above.

"It is not an ancient book that needs to be elucidated for the present day, but the present that needs to be elucidated in the light of an ancient book."[15]

VIOLENCE, WAR AND NATIONHOOD

John H. Yoder has rightly noted that the establishment of the church in its sixteenth-century form, which depended on a relationship to political structures, has been replaced not by independence but by a new kind of establishment, conformity to school, job market and media—or as one might put it in light of Clines's comment, conformity to liberal Western values. "Christians in the first century were a minority in a hostile world. Their ethical views were attuned to that context. In the twentieth century Christians . . . are also in a minority in a world committed to other loyalties, yet we do not reason as the early Christians did."[16]

Yoder sees the church's abandonment of pacifism as an instance of that process, but the opposite is nearer the truth. As Clines notes, a preoccupation with the wrongness of violence is a feature of modern liberal Western thinking. Its background in liberal thinking does not make it wrong; it may be a piece of wisdom in our context. But surely no modern Western values are absolutes that provide the basis for our interpretation of Scripture. One could be tempted to make the principle of hardness of heart the key to understanding violence and war in the two Testaments, but that principle does not actually work very well. Insofar as the Bible is concerned about violence, its framework for talking about it differs from the Western one, which does not instinctively distinguish between right and wrong violence. The notion of violence needs nuancing.[17] There is right and wrong violence in Scripture.[18] In the Bible, violence (right violence) was built into God's

---

[15]James Barr, as quoted by Nicholas Lash, *Theology on the Way to Emmaeus* (London: SCM, 1986), p. 55.

[16]John H. Yoder, *The Priestly Kingdom* (Notre Dame: University of Notre Dame Press, 1984), pp. 22-28, 135.

[17]Something similar applies to the notion of genocide: Amos 1–2 suggests that Amos would condemn it, but it is unlikely that he would suggest indicting Joshua for war crimes, or that the New Testament would do so (see Acts 7:45; Heb 11:32-34). See further my discussion of "What About the Canaanites?" in *Old Testament Theology* (Downers Grove, IL: IVP Academic, 2009), 3:569-82.

[18]This is a problem with Stephen N. Williams's otherwise illuminating comments about violence in Joshua in J. Gordon McConville and Stephen N. Williams, *Joshua*, The Two Horizons Old Testament Commentary (Grand Rapids: Eerdmans, 2010), pp. 120-24, where he lumps together the violence over which God grieves in Genesis and the violence that God elsewhere commissions

creation purpose. God's reason for creating humanity was for humanity to exercise rule by force (*rādâ*; Gen 1:26). If we were in any doubt about that verb's connotations, then God's commission to humanity removes such doubts, because God declares that human beings are to subdue the earth (*kābaš*; Gen 1:28); the word denotes forced subjection. Yet there is a difference between such use of force and the violence that Genesis goes on to describe in the stories of Cain and Lamek (Gen 4; cf. the use of the word *ḥāmās* in Gen 6:11-13, though the word may there denote violation in a broader sense). God's proper violence is then a response to improper human violence; it is in this sense that "if there were no human violence, there would be no divine violence."[19] While the First Testament often explicitly or implicitly rules out violent action, the basis on which it then does so is that Israel in its feebleness needs to trust in God rather than take responsibility for its destiny.[20]

Whereas the New Testament has much to say about slavery and marriage, and what it says can seem embarrassing, it has little to say about being a nation or about being an imperial power.[21] That omission can also seem unfortunate, though one might guess at possible reasons. Jesus is aware that he doesn't know when the last day will come, and he doesn't focus much on what may happen in the time that will elapse in between; it's simply a time of waiting (the comment in 2 Pet 3:8-10 and its broader context fill out the point). Related to this fact is the way Jesus doesn't see the life of nations as very significant. It's just a tale of wars and rumors of wars. This attitude could also mean he wouldn't need to focus on what it means to be a nation or an imperial power. It wasn't ultimately important.

Another reason is that in his day the people of God, the Jewish people, is neither an independent nation nor an imperial power, and the group he mostly teaches, his disciples, are not people who would be exercising power if

---

or undertakes. The former is *ḥāmās*, illegitimate violence; the latter is not. In the First Testament, *ḥāmās* "is never predicated of YHWH; so reference to 'YHWH's violence' is in a sense improper" within this frame of reference (Rob Barrett, *Disloyalty and Destruction* [New York: T & T Clark, 2009], p. 58).

[19]Terence E. Fretheim, "God and Violence in the Old Testament, *Word and World* 24 (2004): 18-28 (p. 21).

[20]Cf. John H. Yoder's own study in *The Politics of Jesus*, 2nd ed. (Grand Rapids: Eerdmans, 1994), pp. 76-88.

[21]Cf. O'Donovan's comments in *The Desire of Nations*, p. 219.

it were. Meir Pa'il, an Israeli brigade commander and politician, has noted that
the State of Israel and the Israeli Defense Forces reject the notion of "an eye
for an eye" in the sense of "murder and crude retribution."[22] In a response,
Milton Himmelfarb noted "the difference between the moral problems that
Pa'il was considering and those which concern Jews in the Diaspora. Jews who
are living only as individuals within a larger society have, at most, the moral
problems of individuals." The problems of Jews in Israel are of quite a different
scope.[23] The bumper sticker says, "When Jesus said, 'Love your enemies,' I
think he probably meant don't kill them." It might seem surprising that he did
not make the comment "It was said of old, 'You shall only make war when
God tells you to do so,' but I say to you, 'You shall not make war at all.'" But
the question of disciples making war did not arise in his or their context.

On History and Politics

What is true about Jesus' teaching is also true elsewhere in the New Testament,
which doesn't focus much on the way history and politics may unfold before
Jesus' final "appearing." There is thus no raw material from the New Testament
for approving or disapproving the state's involvement in violence, except
perhaps in Romans 13. John Yoder argues that in this chapter, bearing the sword
refers to a judicial and police function, not to executing the death penalty or
making war.[24] This distinction seems alien and anachronistic.[25] Yoder is right
that it was secular sources that provided later Christian thinkers with the way
of thinking that led to the just war tradition; it does not follow what Jesus said
about loving enemies and "the norm of the cross and the life of Jesus Christ as
the way of dealing with conflict."[26] The problem is that there was no raw material from the New Testament for any understanding of the state, which is one
reason why Christians turned to the secular just war tradition when they found
themselves involved in governing nations and empires. Yoder goes on, "The
new stance . . . assigns to civil government . . . a role in carrying out God's will
that is quite incompatible with the fruit of the progressive relativization of

---

[22]Meir Pa'il, "The Dynamics of Power," in *Modern Jewish Ethics*, ed. Marvin Fox (Columbus: Ohio
    State University Press, 1975), pp. 191-220 (p. 193).
[23]As related in Fox, "A Response to Meir Pa'il," in *Modern Jewish Ethics*, pp. 221-27 (p. 221).
[24]Yoder, *The Politics of Jesus*, p. 203.
[25]Cf. O'Donovan, *The Desire of Nations*, p. 152.
[26]Yoder, *The Priestly Kingdom*, p. 75.

kingship from Samuel to Jeremiah to Jesus and Jochanan ben Zakkai" (who sought to make peace with the Roman forces during the siege of Jerusalem).[27] "The two ancient turning points represented by Jeremiah and Constantine have become . . . the two most important landmarks outside the New Testament itself for clarifying what is at stake in the Christian faith."[28]

On this view, Jeremiah does not see the coming downfall of Judah as marking a scattering that constitutes a hiatus after which normalcy will return. In his letter to the exiles in Babylon (Jer 29), Yoder says,

> God instructed the people in Babylon to stay there, to renounce notions of an early return to Judaea, to settle in . . . and (especially) to "seek the welfare of the city where I have sent you into exile. . . ." The move to Babylon was not a two-generation parenthesis, after which the Davidic or Solomonic project was supposed to take up again where it had left off. It was rather the beginning . . . of a new phase of the Mosaic project.[29]

The Jeremianic model (Yoder believes) turns Jews into a people who do not seek to take control of history. Christian pacifism follows that stance.[30]

This reading of the First Testament in general and of Jeremiah in particular is open to a series of objections. The clearest is that Jeremiah makes explicit that the move to Babylon was indeed a two-generation parenthesis. He is unambiguous that the exiles are to settle down for seventy years, after which Yahweh will bring them back to their land (Jer 29:10-14), and elsewhere he is explicit that Yahweh will "raise up for David a faithful branch, and he will reign as king, act wisely and implement faithful government in the land" (Jer 23:5-6). While Jeremiah indeed had no time for the idea that the Judahites would take control of history, this stance was not a novel one. Kingship was already relativized by Samuel, yet it was allowed; it is hard to see any difference in Jeremiah. While there are psalms that speak of the Davidic king as Yahweh's agent in ruling the world, they give little indication of seeing this vision as a political program, and none of the prophets before Jeremiah any more than afterwards articulated an expectation along those lines. It's harder to say whether Jeremiah would regard Ezra and Nehemiah

---

[27]Ibid.
[28]John H. Yoder, *For the Nations* (Grand Rapids: Eerdmans, 1997), p. 8.
[29]Ibid., p. 53.
[30]Ibid., pp. 66-70.

as inappropriate "deviations from the Jeremiah line," as people "politicking for imperial authorization."[31] What is clear is that their stories are part of the Scriptures and that the Scriptures are not uneasy with their stance. Their needing to deal with the question of relations with the secular powers makes them a significant resource for the people of God when they need to do so. One might also see it as significant that the stance of the Maccabees is not represented within the Scriptures.

On Waiting and Working for the Kingdom

Between David's day and Jesus' day a thousand years passed. Since Jesus' day, twice as much time has passed. During these two millennia, millions of believers in Jesus have lived as members of independent nations and of imperial powers, often ruling them and thus controlling their national and imperial policies, or at least taking part in democratic processes whereby they chose people to determine these policies, and thus sharing in responsibility for them. For the first two or three centuries after Jesus, in the Roman Empire the question of being a Christian politician or ruler could hardly arise. The turning point was indeed the reign of Constantine, who mercifully turned the empire from one that persecuted and martyred believers into one that recognized Christian faith and even made it the empire's official though not exclusive religion.[32] There thus comes about an alliance between empire and church, an alliance with potential as well as danger. Both the potential and the danger are realized over subsequent centuries. If Constantine was concerned to control the church, it was at least in part with a concern about a question such as, "How can I get two North African Churches that hate each other enough to kill to recognize each other as brothers?"[33]

We have noted in chapter two that while the teaching of Jesus and of the New Testament has some significance for both empire and church in this situation, the more obvious and immediate scriptural material for the instruction of empire and church comes in the First Testament. It comes in the way the First Testament speaks of Yahweh's attitude to Assyria, Babylon,

---

[31]Ibid., p. 74.

[32]Our main source for a knowledge of Constantine is the glowing account of *The Life of Constantine* by Eusebius, the Bishop of Caesarea, who was born slightly before him but outlived him by two or three years.

[33]Peter J. Leithart, *Defending Constantine* (Downers Grove, IL: InterVarsity Press, 2010), p. 157.

Persia and Greece, and in the broader way it speaks of Yahweh's attitude to Israel, which for much of the time is both a political entity and the people of God. One key facet of this dynamic is the relationship of kings, priests and prophets. It is possible for the emperor to want to control the church and for Henry VIII to declare himself head of the church, but it is possible for Athanasius to resist Constantine (even if Athanasius did pay for his resistance) and for Ambrose to rebuke Theodosius.

Constantinianism is a heresy if it implies the claim that the Christian empire can be identified with the kingdom of God and be the fulfillment of scriptural prophecies of the messianic age. But it is just as questionable to argue that "the alternative to resigning ourselves to exile without end . . . is the narrative of history, and of our lives in history, moving toward the Kingdom of God. . . . This is, to be sure, the Christian narrative."[34] How do we look at things when the end did not come? Are we simply left to our own devices? Or is the transition to Christendom the way God chose to work? Or do we deny history? "The common Christian calling is a project: i.e., a goal-oriented movement through time," Yoder argues.[35] Jesus is a charter to which further development must be faithful and by which it will be evaluated, as history moves on from the New Testament; "renewed recourse to the New Testament . . . enables authentic progress."[36]

There is no basis in Scripture for the conviction that the narrative of history is moving toward the kingdom of God. Nor does a consideration of the narrative of history over the past two thousand years offer any pointers in that direction. Jesus rather speaks of wars and rumors of wars, and the New Testament envisages that later times will see apostasy and heresy (1 Tim 4:1-2). As we have noted in chapter two, bringing in the kingdom of God is fortunately God's business.

In chapter six I noted that my stepdaughter and her husband are spending their lives working for an antigenocide movement. Yesterday I plucked up the courage to ask her whether she thought the movement would ever succeed, implicitly raising the question whether they were wasting their lives. She had thought about the question and knew that they were unlikely

---

[34]Richard John Neuhaus, *American Babylon* (New York: Basic, 2009), p. 163.
[35]Yoder, *The Priestly Kingdom*, p. 3.
[36]Yoder, *For the Nations*, pp. 139-40.

to achieve their aim, but she drew an analogy with the antislavery movement. It had not eliminated slavery; there is still slavery in the world. But it had made slavery an unacceptable notion. Their aim in the antigenocide movement was to make genocide an unacceptable notion. Perhaps it is a possibility; certainly it's worth aiming to get governments that want to be part of the "world community" to foreswear and oppose genocide as they foreswear and oppose slavery. It's an aim that's in keeping with other aspects of our seeking to restrain the outworking of sinfulness in the world. But it's not the bringing in of the reign of justice and righteousness. I am even more proud and enthusiastic in connection with the energy Katie-Jay and Gabriel put into seeking to bring healing and love and a sense of recognition to the refugees themselves and their children who have known nothing but life in a camp. That work does look like the bringing in of a reign of justice and righteousness in these people's lives.

9

Theological Interpretation:

Don't Be Christ-Centered, Don't Be Trinitarian, Don't Be Constrained by the Rule of Faith

The New Testament assumes that the First Testament Scriptures will be useful for Christian faith and life, but Christians often have a hard time with the idea. One reason for this difficulty that has underlain much of this book is that a selective use of the New Testament makes it possible to formulate a version of biblical faith that is more congenial to Western Christians than one that reflects the Scriptures more broadly. Another reason is the fact that scholarly study of the First Testament over the past century or two has seemed at best uninteresting. The fact that history was so important in the context of modernity made it inevitable that the focus of scholarly study became the tracing of the historical realities behind the biblical text. There were two drawbacks to that quest. One was that it produced no clear results. The other was that it produced nothing that helped people interact with the First Testament as Scripture, as writings with something to say to us that might be useful for Christian faith and life.

HISTORICAL AND THEOLOGICAL INTERPRETATION

Enter "theological interpretation," which became a growth industry at the beginning of the twenty-first century. While I am troubled by assumptions adopted by many of its advocates, especially regarding the First Testament, I am enthusiastic about interpretation of Scripture that is theological and not merely historical. Indeed, I regret the need to argue for it. One of the main reasons why the documents in the Bible exist and why they are present in the Bible is that they talk about God and people. Their speaking about God and people emerges from historical contexts and often involves referring to historical events, so that investigating these contexts and events contributes to an understanding of the writings. Further, a book such as Genesis or Isaiah came into existence by a complex historical process over a number of centuries, and discovering the nature of this process can contribute to our understanding the eventual form of the books. But the problem with the rigorous scholarly study of the past two centuries is that it has largely confined itself to investigating these questions concerning the historical events the documents refer to and the historical process whereby they came into being. It has not been so interested in going on to read the documents for themselves in light of this historical study.

The basis for my concern about this narrow focus of scholarly study is not merely that I view these writings as Scripture. A broader consideration is involved. This scholarly work presents itself as objective study of the documents, which as such seeks to get at their own agenda, but it has actually not taken account of their own nature. It has ignored a key feature that lies at the center of that agenda, their religious and theological concern. The focus on historical events and processes was decided by the critical approach itself, not by the text. This focus would be unobjectionable if critical study recognized the fact and acknowledged that it was using the text out of an interest different from the text's own. But it commonly does not do so. The problem with historical-critical exegesis is that it is not critical enough.[1] As is the case in connection with ethics, it is not self-critical; it does not consider the way its own agenda skews its study.

WHAT IS AN INTERPRETER TRYING TO DO?

Historical-critical study illustrates how any interpretive undertaking is affected by the questions, interests and commitments with which we come to texts. It

---

[1]Cf. Karl Barth's prefaces in *The Epistle to the Romans* (reprinted Oxford: Oxford University Press, 1963). Thomas A. Bennett notes some ways in which critical methods can feed into theological interpretation in "Paul Ricoeur and the Hypothesis of the Text in Theological Interpretation," *Journal of Theological Interpretation* 5 (2011): 211-29.

is not merely that historical-critical study is influenced by evolutionism, Hegelianism, rationalism and romanticism, though the study is so influenced.[2] It is that the very focus on historical questions has a decisive affect on what interpreters find in the books, with the problem that it corresponds only partially to the book's own interests. It is as if one studied Shakespeare's *Anthony and Cleopatra* by focusing on what it reveals about the Roman Empire or about England in the seventeenth century, or studied *Henry VIII* in order to trace the process whereby John Fletcher may have collaborated in writing the play or may have revised it. Such questions do not provide the keys to opening up Shakespeare's plays, and neither do they fulfill this end for the First Testament.

In reading Shakespeare, or Plato, we may think about what their works tell us about their times, but we do not focus primarily on that question; or at least, we do not assume that such study counts as interpreting Shakespeare or Plato. We treat them as texts, as works. We ask about their structure, about the way their plot develops, and about the ideas they put forward. It is possible to refer to such a reading of Scripture as a "canonical" one, but "canonical" interpretation has many different meanings, even for its foremost advocate.[3] Further, it is inclined to suggest confessional and churchly; canonical interpretation is important for people who want to read Isaiah "as Scripture." In reading Shakespeare for its structure and ideas, we do not see ourselves as involved in canonical or final-form or synchronic or theological interpretation. It is just—interpretation. Even if one is reading the Hebrew Bible as an artifact as opposed to reading it as Scripture,[4] one ought to give some priority to reading it for its own agenda.

That agenda centers on questions about God and Israel and life. The writings are designed to shape people's relationship with God and Israel and life. They are religious literature, not merely history or sociology. Exegetes need not agree with what the texts have to say on these matters, or even on whether these questions are important, but if they are aiming to do exegesis,

---

[2]Cf. R. J. Thompson, *Moses and the Law in a Century of Criticism Since Graf* (Leiden: Brill, 1970), pp. 35-48.

[3]Contrast different works by Brevard S. Childs: e.g., *Biblical Theology in Crisis* (Philadelphia: Westminster, 1970); *Introduction to the Old Testament as Scripture* (Philadelphia: Fortress, 1979); *Old Testament Theology in a Canonical Context* (Philadelphia: Fortress, 1986).

[4]See Benjamin D. Sommer, "Dialogical Biblical Theology," in *Biblical Theology: Introducing the Conversation*, ed. Leo G. Perdue, Robert Morgan and Benjamin D. Sommer (Nashville: Abingdon, 2009), pp. 1-53 (p. 14).

one would expect that they would give major attention to these questions. Theological interpretation reasserts this point that should be self-evident on the basis of the nature of the literature.

Even advocates of theological interpretation do not make this point sharply enough if they declare that theological interpretation involves going beyond historical exegesis in order to look at the text in light of a theological perspective that includes what we know about God as a whole.[5] Historical exegesis will itself be theological, in the sense of reflecting on the theological questions that are inherent in the texts. Thus Brevard Childs in his commentary on Isaiah makes the point that the book of Isaiah is about divine realities, not about human faith. Isaiah 1, for instance, focuses not on Isaiah the prophet nor primarily on Israel but on God—God's anger, God's efforts to win the people back, God's punishment, God's restoration. Regarding Isaiah 40:12-31, Childs comments that the text's focus "does not revolve around the anthropocentric complaints of Israel, but rather the focus is unremittingly theocentric."[6] One could extend the point to Scripture as a whole.

Theological interpretation is proper exegesis. In light of that understanding I want to make three points in relation to current views about theological interpretation.

Theological but not Christocentric

The opening page of the main text in a book on theological interpretation of the First Testament declares that "any theological hermeneutic worth its salt must be Christocentric."[7] My response is that on the contrary, theological interpretation needs to be theocentric. A theological commentary on Jonah declares, "The book of Jonah is all about Christ."[8] I am not sure what this statement means, and the commentary does not go far in clarifying the point,[9] but while it would be meaningful to suggest that all of Jonah helps

---

[5]See, e.g., Matthew Levering, *Ezra & Nehemiah* (Grand Rapids: Brazos, 2007), p. 22; also his *Participatory Biblical Exegesis* (Notre Dame: University of Notre Dame, 2008), p. 61.

[6]Brevard S. Childs, *Isaiah* (Louisville: Westminster John Knox, 2001), pp. 17, 307.

[7]Craig G. Bartholomew, "Listening for God's Address," in *Hearing the Old Testament*, ed. Craig G. Bartholomew and David J. H. Beldman (Grand Rapids: Eerdmans, 2012), pp. 3-19 (p. 3).

[8]Phillip Cary, *Jonah*, The Brazos Theological Commentary on the Bible (Grand Rapids: Brazos, 2008), p. 17.

[9]The comments about Jesus include that Jesus contrasts with Jonah in his obedience to God's call (p. 40), identifies with Jonah (p. 45) and sleeps in a boat like Jonah (p. 50).

us understand Christ, as far as what the book itself is "about," it would be more appropriate to say that the book of Jonah is all about God.

The New Testament itself has a variety of lenses for looking at the First Testament. Christians are inclined to assume that *the* point about the First Testament is its witness to Jesus. The New Testament has a broader view. It has many other lenses—it uses the First Testament for insight on the church, the ministry, mission, the world and so on. "Paul sees the fulfillment of prophecy not primarily in events in the life of Jesus (as Matthew does) but in God's gathering of a church composed of Jews and Gentiles together," so that "his hermeneutic is functionally ecclesiocentric rather than christocentric."[10] "Remarkably little of his interpretive practice bears a christocentric stamp." His theme is that "the gospel is the fulfillment, not the negation, of God's word to Israel."[11] One could say that Paul's interpretation, as well as being church-centered, is Israel-centered, like the First Testament itself.

It might be argued that the entirety of the New Testament's theological interpretation is in some sense christological, but it is not christocentric. Yet even if it were, that fact would not mean that all interpretation should be so. I do not imply that the New Testament might be wrong in being christocentric, only that there could be good reasons for its being christocentric; its vocation would then be to offer an interpretation of Jesus. But the New Testament itself shows that an interpretation of Jesus is not the only focus of interpretation that the church needs. Further, interpretation of Jesus with the aid of the First Testament is a different exercise from understanding what God was doing in speaking to Israel through the First Testament writers, and thus understanding what God has to say to us through their work. Matthew's account of Jesus' birth does not help one understand the passage in Isaiah 7 about a girl having a baby. Theological interpretation of Isaiah 7 will need to look at what God was saying to Israel in that passage. It will not need to refer to Jesus.

One of my students once astutely reversed my question about lenses,

---

[10]Richard B. Hays, *Echoes of Scripture in the Letters of Paul* (New Haven: Yale University Press, 1989), p. xiii. Cf. Stephen Fowl, *Engaging Scripture* (Oxford: Blackwell, 1998), p. 152. Hays later (pp. 98-99) notes that the hermeneutic of Hebrews is "relentlessly christocentric"; this is one way of articulating the perspective that has led to its opening itself to the misreading I considered in chapter five. But Hays later repented: see "'Here We Have No Lasting City,'" in *The Epistle to the Hebrews and Christian Theology*, ed. Richard Bauckham et al. (Grand Rapids: Eerdmans, 2009), pp. 151-73 (pp. 151-52).
[11]Hays, *Echoes of Scripture*, pp. 84, 34; see further pp. 84-121.

asking what lenses the First Testament provides for looking at the New. In a sense the question is anachronistic, but it is illuminating. The main answer is that the First Testament's lens is God. The First Testament restrains christocentric interpretation of either Testament. It draws our attention to the fact that Christ is not christocentric. "Christ was theocentric."[12] He came to speak of God's reign. At the End he will give up the reign to God, "so that God may be all in all" (1 Cor 15:24, 28). When every knee bows to Jesus, it will be "to the glory of God the Father" (Phil 2:11). Jürgen Moltmann has observed that "the name the church gives itself" is "the church of Jesus Christ."[13] This name is not the one the New Testament gives it. The New Testament never describes the church as the church of Jesus Christ, only as the church of God. George S. Hendry declared that "the Holy Spirit is in an exclusive sense the Spirit of Christ."[14] But the expression "Spirit of Christ" comes only twice in the New Testament (Rom 8:9; 1 Pet 1:11; "Spirit of Jesus" comes twice more, in Acts 16:7; Phil 1:19), whereas "Spirit of God" comes twelve times, and of course many times in the First Testament.[15]

According to Francis Watson, "Christian faith is . . . necessarily christocentric: for in Jesus Christ the identity of God, the creator who is also the God of Israel, is definitively disclosed in the triune name of Father, Son and Holy Spirit for the salvation of humankind."[16] Robert Wall puts it another way: "The truth about God is now known more completely because of Jesus Christ in whom God's word and purposes became flesh and through whom God's grace and truth are mediated to us."[17]

Yet in what sense is the truth about God known more completely through Jesus? As evidence for this statement Robert Wall refers to John 1:14, which declares that Jesus was full of grace and truth. But John does not mean that before Jesus people did not realize that God was characterized by grace and

---

[12]P. T. Forsyth, *The Justification of God* (New York: Scribner's, 1917), p. 148.

[13]Moltmann, *The Church in the Power of the Spirit* (New York: Harper and Row, 1977), p. 66.

[14]George S. Hendry, *The Holy Spirit in Christian Theology*, rev. ed. (Philadelphia: Westminster, 1965), p. 26; cf. Michael E. Lodahl, *Shekhinah Spirit* (Mahwah, NJ: Paulist, 1992), p. 26.

[15]Hendry leaves these Old Testament occurrences out of account on the grounds that the New Testament ignores them; he does not think that the New Testament as a whole accepts the inspiration of the Old Testament as a whole (*The Holy Spirit in Christian Theology*, pp. 27-29).

[16]Francis Watson, *Text and Truth* (Grand Rapids: Eerdmans, 1997), p. 185.

[17]Robert W. Wall, "Reading the Bible from Within Our Traditions," in *Between Two Horizons*, ed. Joel B. Green and Max Turner (Grand Rapids: Eerdmans, 2000), pp. 88-107 (p. 91).

truth. The very words are picked up from God's self-revelation at Sinai. John's point is not that no one knew God's nature before Jesus but that the known nature of God was embodied in Jesus. Robert Wall also refers to Hebrews 1:1-2; we have noted in chapter 5 that its implications are similar.

Jesus did not reveal something new about God. What he did was embody God. The point about Jesus was not something new that he revealed. It was something that he was and did. In embodying God's instinct to sacrifice himself for people, which God had been showing through Israel's story, Jesus made it possible for God's grace and truth to take hold of us. Before Jesus, Israel had a perfectly good revelation of God. The problem was that people did not give a proper response to this revelation. Jesus came to make such a response possible. If this is the sense in which theological interpretation needs to be christocentric, then one can affirm it. But it does not bring a new meaning to First Testament texts.

Francis Watson, again, declares, "The Old Testament comes to us with Jesus and from Jesus, and can never be understood in abstraction from him." There can be "no interpretative programmes that assume an autonomous Old Testament." It is "a body of texts whose centre and goal lie not in themselves but in that towards which they are retrospectively seen to be oriented." "The Christian church has not received an Old Testament that can be abstracted from Jesus. Such a collection would not be an 'Old Testament.'" Letting it be autonomous excludes or minimizes the "hermeneutical significance of the event of the Word made flesh."[18]

But one flaw in this argument is that the Scriptures that come to us with Jesus and from Jesus are not the Old Testament. They are simply the Scriptures. They did not become "the Old Testament" until a century or two after Jesus' day.[19] I am not sure what would be the unfortunate result of interpretive programs that assume an autonomous Old Testament. Our actual problem is that of subsuming the First Testament under our understanding of what is Christian, so that this strategy enables us to sidestep parts of the First Testament that we want to avoid. By sleight of hand, aspects of what the First Testament says about God are filtered out in the name of christo-

---

[18]Watson, *Text and Truth*, pp. 182-83; the first quotation is italicized. On p. 185 he is explicit that he calls for "christocentric" interpretation.
[19]See the note at the end of the introduction to this volume.

centric interpretation. But the real problem is that we don't like these aspects of the Scriptures. Christocentric interpretation makes it harder for the Scriptures to confront us when we need to be confronted. It is not the case that what was hidden in the Old is revealed in the New.[20] Rather, there are many things revealed in the First Testament that the church has hidden by its interpretive strategy, obscuring the nature of scriptural faith.

Here are some examples.[21] First, the First Testament has a huge amount to say about superpowers: Assyria, Babylon, Persia and Greece. If the church had read what it says, it might have been able to argue against some of the oppressiveness of what we British did in creating our empire and what the United States has done as a superpower, and to avoid getting sucked into confusing its mission with the imperial project. Second, the First Testament has a huge amount to say about work. One of its assumptions is that work is central to family life and the family is a key structure for work, while "employment" (selling your labor to someone outside the family) is a marginal and rather odd business. Third, Christians have often held an oppressive understanding of the relationship of husbands to their wives. A christocentric or christological interpretation of the Song of Songs prevents the application of that book to the formulating of a vision for relationships between a man and a woman. An autonomous First Testament affirms the sexual relationship between a man and a woman in a way the New Testament does not.

Could an autonomous First Testament encourage the kind of genocide that Deuteronomy and Joshua speak of? The First Testament itself does not treat such genocide as a pattern for regular Israelite life,[22] any more than mainstream Jewish interpretation does.[23] Further, ironically, the positive way the New Testament speaks in Acts 7:45 about Joshua's taking the land

---

[20]"Et in Vetere Novum lateat, et in Novo Vetus pateat" (Augustine, *Quaestionum in Heptateuchum Libri Septem* 2.73 [col. 0623], in a comment on Ex 20:19).

[21]See further my *Old Testament Theology*, 3 vols. (Downers Grove, IL: IVP Academic, 2003-2009).

[22]Which raises the possibility that for the Old Testament Joshua is already "noninstrumentalisable" if not quite "heretical, subversive and disowned"—that is, it is respected and recognized but not exactly "used" (Douglas S. Earl, *Reading Joshua as Christian Scripture* [Winona Lake, IN: Eisenbrauns, 2010], pp. 4-6, quoting from Jan Assmann, *Religion and Cultural Memory* [Stanford: Stanford University Press, 2006], p. 27).

[23]See, e.g., Elliot N. Dorff, *To Do the Right and the Good* (Philadelphia: Jewish Publication Society, 2002), pp. 161-83.

and in Hebrews 11 about Israel conquering kingdoms, becoming faithful in battle and routing foreign armies suggests that it did not feel any of the unease about such First Testament narratives that is characteristic of modern Christians, as it does not feel any unease about the kind of praying that occurs in Psalm 137.[24] But in any case, passages about genocide and imprecatory psalms are an odd starting point for thinking about the theological interpretation of the First Testament. "It is . . . not the difficult passages that provide the critical norm for biblical interpretation."[25] One would not start from the passage about the millennium in Revelation 20 in seeking to understand New Testament interpretation. (That, of course, is a joke, because it is what some people in the United States do.) Yet the fact that passages such as those in Joshua and Psalms strike us as difficult texts may itself help us to see some of the issues involved in theological interpretation of the First Testament.

While I do not see much danger in an autonomous First Testament, I see much danger in the narrowing down of the First Testament's agenda to that of a Christian tradition that is itself narrower even than that of the New Testament. Christocentric interpretation makes it harder for the Scriptures to confront us when we need to be confronted.

THEOLOGICAL BUT NOT TRINITARIAN

"Precisely because a theological hermeneutic is Christocentric it will be trinitarian."[26] This assertion is open to similar questioning as applies to the idea that it should be christocentric, and to some further questioning of its own.

Admittedly, the notion that theological interpretation should be trinitarian seems to be more a theoretical principle than one with significant purchase in connection with actual texts. Perhaps it is mainly a declaration of the truth that we interpret Scripture knowing that the real God who is Father, Son and Holy Spirit is the one to whom the First Testament refers. God has indeed been Trinity from the Beginning, and all God's activity in

---

[24]Earl begins his study *Reading Joshua as Christian Scripture* by noting that unease about Joshua became prevalent only in the late twentieth century (pp. 2-3), though he also notes that it was felt by people such as Marcion, Valentinus and Basilides, and thus by Origen, though not by Augustine (p. 9).

[25]Levering, *Participatory Biblical Exegesis*, p. 81.

[26]Bartholomew, "Listening for God's Address," p. 4.

the First Testament is the activity of the trinitarian God, even though the
First Testament itself does not say so.[27]

> All Christian use of the Old Testament seems to depend on the belief that the
> One God who is the God of Israel is also the God and Father of Jesus Christ.
> All our use of the Old Testament goes back to this belief. What is said there
> that relates to "God" relates to our God. Consequently that which can be
> known of our God is known only when we consider the Old Testament as a
> place in which he is known.[28]

An instance of trinitarian theological interpretation of particular texts is
the suggestion that God's being Trinity enables one to see extra significance
in the way the prophets speak of the Father, the Messiah and the spirit of God.

> The Major Prophets . . . are strikingly trinitarian. First of all, their message is
> christocentric, repeatedly looking beyond the ongoing series of political and
> military crises and the spiritual malaise that marked the Israelite monarchy,
> as well as the devastating humiliation of exile, to the coming of a Davidic heir
> and just ruler who would succeed where his predecessors had failed and
> would therefore enable Israel to experience the covenantal blessings that they
> frequently forfeited through disobedience. . . .
>
> Second, the Major Prophets refer more frequently to God as "Father" than
> other sections of the Old Testament (e.g., Isa. 9:6; 63:16; 64:8; Jer. 3:4, 19; cf. Mal.
> 1:6; 2:10). Finally, the Spirit is instrumentally involved in the ministries of the
> prophets and the future Davidic king (e.g., Isa. 11:2; 32:15; 34:16; 42:1; 44:3; 48:16;
> 59:21; 61:1; 63:10, 11, 14; Ezek. 2:2; 3:12, 14, 24; 8:3; 11:1, 5, 24; 36:27; 37:1, 14; 39:29;
> 43:5). The Major Prophets should be heard as a message regarding the triune
> God's will and plan for humanity—with a special focus on Israel.[29]

There are two sorts of problems with that quotation. It is insufficiently theological, and it skews insight into the theological meaning of the prophets.

---

[27]I take this to be part of Levering's point in his advocacy of "participatory exegesis." He argues that
"the texts and their authors are already historically caught up in a participatory relationship . . . with
the trans-temporal realities of faith." Thus "the Church's theological and metaphysical 'reading into'
biblical texts may largely be expected to *illumine* the realities described in Scripture" (*Participatory
Biblical Exegesis*, p. 5; his emphasis). My gloss would be that it indeed illumines the realities; it does
not illumine the texts, and it may obscure them and thus ultimately obscure the realities, too.

[28]James Barr, *Old and New in Interpretation* (New York: Harper, 1966), p. 149; cf. Bartholomew,
"Listening for God's Address," p. 8.

[29]Richard Schultz, "Hearing the Major Prophets," in Bartholomew and Beldman, *Hearing the Old
Testament*, pp. 332-55 (pp. 335-36).

With regard to the references to the coming Davidic ruler: first, the prophets do not repeatedly look to such a person. There are relatively few such references (e.g., Is 11:1-10; Jer 23:5-6; Ezek 34:23-24). There are other texts that the New Testament uses to help it understand Jesus, such as the passage about a young girl in Isaiah 7, and other texts that the Christian tradition came to use in that way, such as the "to us a child is born" passage in Isaiah 9, but if we take those later allusions as key to understanding the prophets, we commit two evils (as Jer 2:13 puts it). We lose the inherent theological significance of what God was saying through the prophets to their people, and we gain nothing in its place, because whatever we are reading into the prophets' words we already know from the New Testament and the Christian tradition. Further, by focusing on the passages referring to a coming Davidic ruler, we obscure the theological significance of this very expectation. It is only one aspect of the way the prophets portray God's fulfilling his purpose, and it is part of a broader picture. When the prophets refer to this future consummation, they more often do so without referring to a Davidic ruler (so, for instance, throughout Is 40–66). Now, all God's promises find their Yes in Christ (2 Cor 1:20). So focusing on the promises that explicitly relate to a Davidic ruler obscures the way Jesus is the fulfillment or confirmation of all God's promises.

With regard to the references to God as Father, there are two parallel points to be made. One is that the prophets' references relate to God's being the Father of Israel, whereas in connection with trinitarian interpretation, the point about God's being Father is that he is the Father of the Son. Further, the God who is called Father in the First Testament is not simply the first person of the Trinity. Yahweh is God—period; therefore Yahweh is Father, Son and Spirit.[30] Applying prophetic passages about the Father to the first person of the Trinity obscures their theological significance.

Further, again, the Christian idea of God's fatherhood in relation to his people is more often conveyed in the First Testament by images other than fatherhood. It is a common feature of the relationship between the Testaments that they express the same ideas but use different images for them.

---

[30]Williams declares that "in the New Testament the Lord God of Israel is identified as the Father of Jesus Christ" (J. Gordon McConville and Stephen N. Williams, *Joshua* [Grand Rapids: Eerdmans, 2010], p. 217). This seems an oversimplification in light of the way the New Testament applies passages about Yahweh to Jesus as Lord.

For instance, both Testaments speak of a quasi-personal embodiment of power that is resistant to God. The New Testament often calls this entity Satan. While the First Testament uses the Hebrew word *satan*, it does not use it in that connection; it refers to this entity by terms such as Leviathan. The two Testaments' use of the same word is not always an indication that they are referring to the same reality, and their use of different words is not always an indication that they are referring to different realities. When the First Testament wants to refer to the relationship between God and his people that is conveyed by the image of fatherhood, it more often uses other images. A spectacular example is the image of the *gō'ēl*, the next of kin, guardian, redeemer or restorer. Your *gō'ēl* is someone to whose family you belong who is more powerful than you and who has resources that you do not have, which he is willing to use on your behalf because you are a member of his family. The image overlaps considerably with the New Testament idea of God's fatherhood in relation to his people, but the link is substantial not linguistic.

A focus on explicit First Testament references to God's spirit further obscures an understanding of the activity of the trinitarian God in Israel. Paul declares that the promise of blessing to Abraham is fulfilled in the giving of the Spirit (Gal 3:14).[31] In the New Testament, talk of God's spirit comes to be the dominant way of referring to God's blessing, presence and activity within his people. In the First Testament there are many ways of speaking about God's presence and activity, such as God's hand, God's arm and God's face. Spirit is the New Testament and doctrinal equivalent of all these.[32] The implication is that we can see the presence and activity of the Holy Spirit wherever we see the real and powerful presence of God in the First Testament. If we see the presence and activity of the Spirit only when we find occurrences of the word *rûaḥ*, we miss much. We may infer the activity of the Holy Spirit whenever we find First Testament references to the activity of God's hand, God's arm or God's face, but adopting that understanding involves a theological judgment, not an exegetical one, and it may obscure the point that a particular passage makes. Further, it is misleading to describe that understanding as theological exegesis or theological interpre-

---

[31]Cf. Gordon D. Fee, *God's Empowering Presence* (Peabody, MA: Hendrickson, 1994), p. 811.
[32]See further chapter three above.

tation; it might be better to call it theological translation. This term may recognize the priority of the Scriptures' own way of speaking, rather than seeming to decode it into something else.

Christian theological interpretation will be trinitarian in the sense that it knows that Yahweh the God of Israel is the God who is Trinity. It will not be trinitarian in the sense that it looks for reference to the Trinity in Isaiah or Genesis.

THEOLOGICAL BUT NOT CONSTRAINED BY THE RULE OF FAITH

I have a more general unease about trinitarian interpretation. The doctrine of the Trinity is a piece of church tradition, not part of Scripture. It is a legitimate spelling out of material in the New Testament, and I accept it and say the Creed on Sundays without any mental reservations. But it is a human formulation explicating the scriptural material about God in the context of a particular European philosophical framework in the Mediterranean world in Late Antiquity. It is not part of the New Testament, and there is something odd about treating it as a basis for deciding the meaning of Scripture itself.

Trinitarian thinking has become a focus of theology in the West in recent decades, and the stress on the Trinity in theological interpretation is one aspect of that development. The Trinity appeals to us Westerners because we are desperate to become more relational. In other words, as contextual factors were involved in the formulating of the doctrine of the Trinity, so contextual factors are involved in Western interest in the Trinity and thus in the stress on the Trinity in theological interpretation.

The original formulation of trinitarian doctrine took place in the context of the broader formulating of the framework of Christian faith that is embodied in the creeds. There we declare our faith in God as the Creator, in Christ as the redeemer and in the Holy Spirit as the giver of life. The shape of the creeds corresponds to the outlined understanding of the Christian faith expressed in the ancient Rule of Faith, which follows a narrative line: creation, fall, Jesus, Pentecost, the second coming.

The importance of the Rule of Faith is a significant aspect of recent stress on theological interpretation. According to the editor of the Brazos Theological Commentary on the Bible, a theologian such as Irenaeus thinks that the "the Bible is vast, heterogeneous, full of confusing passages and obscure words, and difficult to understand." It is as if the Scriptures are a collection of tiles designed to be assembled as a mosaic, but without any instructions for their assembly. It is the Rule of Faith that makes it possible to puzzle out the mosaic.[33]

That summary misstates Irenaeus's point in *Against the Heresies* 1.8-10.[34] Indeed, Irenaeus implies the opposite to the idea that the Bible is vast, heterogeneous, full of confusing passages and obscure words, and difficult to understand. He starts from the way the Valentinians get the contents of their faith from outside the Scriptures and then take individual verses and phrases from the Scriptures and string these together so that they seem to support their views, when the compilation actually represents an artificial construct that does not reflect the faith of the Scriptures. They thus "disregard the order and the connection of the Scriptures."[35] Irenaeus goes on nicely to note how one could similarly prove anything to be the teaching of Homer by forming a collection of sayings without regard to their context. In other words, he does not think the Bible is confusing and obscure, but orderly and interconnected. It is not a collection of fragments from which we have to form the big picture. The Bible *is* a big picture, an assembled mosaic. It is the Valentinians who have treated it as a collection of disconnected bits when it is no such thing, and have reassembled it in a different order from its own, utilizing what we would call allegorical method in order to make it say what they believe.

Irenaeus then argues against the Valentinians, not by appealing to the Rule of Faith but by discussing the exegesis of John 1 and showing that the Valentinians' exegesis ignores the contextual meaning of the expressions they pick up. Only after making his exegetical argument, in his next section, does he refer to the Rule of Faith. There he grants that Scripture contains *some* obscurities, for instance in the parables and in the passage about angels that transgressed (2 Pet 2:4), which the Valentinians use to their advantage. He comments that it is when people build doctrines on things that are unclear that they ought rather to rely on the Rule of Faith. He does not set forward the Rule of Faith as a general-purposes guide to the interpretation of Scripture.[36]

---

[33]Russell Reno, in his preface to the Brazos Theological Commentary: e.g., in Levering, *Ezra & Nehemiah*, pp. 9-14 (p. 10).

[34]Tertullian's argument in *Prescription Against Heretics* is similar.

[35]*Against the Heresies* 1.8.1.

[36]Origen does put more emphasis on Scripture's obscurities (see Reno's "Preface," p. 9), but his solution to the problem does not involve interpreting Scripture in light of the Rule of Faith but

"Can and should the Bible be read as a unified story of the triune God's creative and redemptive work?"[37] At the end of his study of "historical criticism in a postmodern age," John J. Collins comments that "the internal pluralism of the Bible, both theological and ethical, has been established beyond dispute,"[38] which implies that we cannot read the Bible as such a unified story. Either we must choose from its different perspectives, or we must impose some unity from outside. My comment is that the appropriate response is rather to deny Collins's premise, or at least to look at the question from the inside of Scripture.[39] Scripture can and should be read as a unified story.

This understanding does not carry with it the implication that (for instance) "the holy land points forward to fulfillment in the body of Christ," either as "the incarnate Son" or "as his body the church."[40] The New Testament contains few direct hints in this direction (Hebrews with its adaptation of the idea of rest is the clearest), though neither does it contain direct hints in another direction. Indeed, the general idea of the First Testament "pointing forward to" or "looking towards" Christ and the New Testament "does not seem to have real meaning."[41] The significance of the motif of land lies elsewhere than in its becoming a metaphor for the body of Christ. Rather, "the contemporary theological relevance of Joshua is unmistakable" because "its central topic of land resonates not only with the modern contention over the territory of Israel-Palestine, but with the perennial relationship between human beings and land, not only as essential to life and sustenance, but also as identity and 'place.'"[42] Relating the motif of land to the body of Christ surrenders its theological potential.

In his introduction to the *Journal of Theological Interpretation,* Joel B. Green observed that "theological interpretation emphasizes the potentially mutual influence of Scripture and doctrine in theological discourse."[43] What is the nature

---

interpreting obscure passages by clear passages: his Jewish teacher had taught him that "the only way to begin to understand them was . . . by means of other passages containing the explanation dispersed throughout them" (p. 32 in the edition of Origen's comments that I have used, *The Philocalia of Origen* [Edinburgh: T & T Clark, 1911], pp. 30-34).

[37]Levering, *Ezra & Nehemiah*, p. 19.

[38]John J. Collins, *The Bible After Babel* (Grand Rapids: Eerdmans, 2005), pp. 160-61.

[39]Cf. Levering, *Ezra and Nehemiah*, p. 19.

[40]Against ibid., p. 125.

[41]Barr, *Old and New in Interpretation*, p. 153.

[42]McConville in McConville and Williams, *Joshua*, p. 11.

[43]Joel B. Green, "The (Re-)Turn to Theology," *Journal of Theological Interpretation* 1 (2007): 1-3 (2).

of that mutual influence? Robert Wall declares that the proper use of Scripture "depends upon interpretation that constrains the theological teaching of a biblical text by the church's 'Rule of Faith.' . . . Scripture is not self-interpreting, then, but is rather rendered coherent and relevant by faithful interpreters whose interpretations are constrained by this Rule." This notion corresponds with the fact that "Scripture was received as God's word by the faith community because its content cohered to the core beliefs of its Christological confession." The First Testament writings so cohered because they had come to be interpreted in a way that meant they did so; the New Testament Scriptures so cohered because this coherence was the basis for their choice.[44]

This comment raises a number of questions. As far as the First Testament is concerned, it is by no means the case that the First Testament Scriptures were received as God's word because their content corresponded to the core beliefs of the church's christological confession. If anything, the process was the opposite. The faith community started off as a Jewish entity that accepted the Jewish Scriptures as God's word and used these Scriptures to help it understand Jesus. The question it had to handle was not whether the Scriptures fitted with Christian faith but whether Christian faith fitted with the Scriptures. Paul knew that if he could not establish this fact, he was in trouble. "The problem of whether the Old Testament was Christian did not arise in the church until the second century A.D. The problem of the first century, and hence of the NT, was whether the NT was biblical."[45] Thus seeing "the New Testament, or more particularly Jesus Christ, as the norm by which the Old is to be measured and interpreted . . . is curious, chiefly because the viewpoint of the earliest Church was exactly the reverse: the Old Testament was the canonical Scripture, the unquestioned authority by which New Testament persons and events were to be assessed."[46]

44Wall, "Reading the Bible from Within Our Traditions," pp. 88, 97, 98. Wall refers directly to Tertullian and quotes his summary of the Rule of Faith, but notes (p. 90) that it is essentially the same as Irenaeus's account.

45James A. Sanders, "Adaptable for Life," in *Magnalia Dei*, ed. F. M. Cross et al., G. E. Wright memorial volume (Garden City, NY: Doubleday, 1976), pp. 531-60 (p. 552).

46David Noel Freedman, in his review of *The Old Testament and Christian Faith*, ed. Bernhard W. Anderson (New York: Harper, 1963), in *Theology Today* 21 (1964-1965): 225-28 (227). In the way it speaks of "the Old Testament" the formulation is slightly anachronistic but not so as to affect the force of the observation; fuzziness over when the Torah, the Prophets and the Writings became a collection that no one would think of augmenting does not affect the fact that the New Testament presupposes the established position of a collection of Scriptures roughly approximate to what later came to be known as "the Old Testament."

It is true that the Rule of Faith provides a horizon from within which we may come to understand the Scriptures, and it may open our eyes to see things within the horizon of the Scriptures themselves. It thus fulfills a function analogous to that of a concern for the gospel's significance for the whole world, which makes it possible to look back at the First Testament and see that this concern is also present there, so that theological interpretation is missional.[47] But its role is to enable us to see things that are there; it does not determine what is allowed to be there.[48] It is not the "definitive hermeneutical framework for understanding the Scriptures."[49] The Scriptures do not need to be rendered coherent and relevant; they are coherent and relevant. The Rule of Faith can help us see how that is so. But where they have a broader horizon than that of the Rule of Faith, we will be wise not to narrow down their horizon to ours; we allow them to broaden our horizon. In practice the church has followed the Rule of Faith in a way that did constrain what the Scriptures are allowed to say, and the Rule of Faith has thus been a disaster for the hearing of the First Testament.[50] The Rule of Faith has no room and no hermeneutic for any episodes in the scriptural story between Genesis 3 and Matthew 1.[51] As Robert W. Jenson put it, "The rule of faith saved the Old Testament as canon for the church—or rather, the church for the Old Testament canon—but in the process it did not open itself to the theological shape of the Old Testament's own narrative, and so it could not support the Old Testament's specific role in the church's practice."[52] One recalls the alleged statement

---

[47]Cf. Christopher J. H. Wright's comment on the missional implications of theological interpretation, in "Mission and Old Testament Interpretation," in Bartholomew and Beldman, *Hearing the Old Testament*, pp. 180-203.

[48]Contrast also Francis Watson's observations about the creeds in *Text, Church and World* (Grand Rapids: Eerdmans, 1994), pp. 5-6.

[49]Against Thomas A. Noble, "The Spirit World," in *The Unseen World*, ed. Anthony N. S. Lane (Grand Rapids: Baker, 1996), pp. 185-223 (p. 190); he claims Calvin's support for this view, but Calvin talks about "some guidance and direction" that will enable people to understand the Scriptures (see the "Subject Matter of the Present Work," the preface to his *Institutes of the Christian Religion*), which is rather different from talk in terms of "definitive."

[50]Contrast the arguments (e.g.) of Robert Wall, "Jesus in the Old Testament," and Kathryn Greene-McCreight, "Sinews Even in Thy Milk," *Journal of Theological Interpretation* 2 (2008): 16-19 and 19-22, that the rule of faith facilitates the interpretation of the First Testament.

[51]Irenaeus does refer to other First Testament material, but not as part of a narrative understanding of Scripture as a whole: see Nathan MacDonald, "Israel and the Old Testament Story in Irenaeus's Presentation of the Rule of Faith," *Journal of Theological Interpretation* 3 (2009): 281-98.

[52]Robert W. Jenson, *Canon and Creed* (Louisville: Westminster John Knox, 2010), p. 29.

about a Vietnamese city by a major in the United States army, that "it became necessary to destroy the town in order to save it."[53]

In critiquing N. T. Wright's work, Richard Hays takes up Wright's claim that he operates purely as a historian and invites him to recognize that he is denying the influence of the fact that he is "a believing Christian, formed intellectually and imaginatively by years of participation in the rich liturgical life of the Church of England; even as a Christian trying to think historically, he is engaged in the project of faith seeking understanding." He goes on to address Wright: "If your reading seems totally unprecedented in the church's whole tradition of reading . . . should that give you pause about whether your interpretation can persuasively claim historical validity?"[54] Wright himself then responds that "to appeal to tradition and dogma as the framework for understanding Jesus is to say that not only the entire enterprise of biblical scholarship but also the entire Protestant Reformation has been based on a mistake." The history of the church does not support the view that tradition has got it mostly right.[55] Theological interpretation needs to pay attention to the Christian tradition in order to broaden the horizon from which it works, but not to subordinate Scripture to the tradition.

It deserves reflection that the interpreters who want to control biblical exegesis by the church's doctrinal tradition are mostly systematic theologians who want to be biblical and the people who want to resist this control are mostly biblical scholars who want to be theological. There are many ways in which questions of power enter into biblical interpretation.

Conclusion

So my argument is that theological interpretation needs to be wary of being christocentric and being Trinitarian and following the formulations of Christian theology and of the Rule of Faith. The God of the First Testament became incarnate in Jesus, but reading the Scriptures, and the First Testament

---

[53]"Ruined Bentre, After 45 Days, Still Awaits Saigon's Aid; Regime Has Offered Nothing in Effort to Rebuild Town," *New York Times*, March 15, 1968 (http://query.nytimes.com/mem/archive/pdf?res=F60716F73A5D147493C7A81788D85F4C8685F9).

[54]Richard B. Hays, "Knowing Jesus," in *Jesus, Paul and the People of God*, ed. Nicholas Perrin and Richard B. Hays (Downers Grove, IL: InterVarsity Press, 2011), pp. 41-61 (pp. 56, 57).

[55]N. T. Wright, "Whence and Whither Historical Jesus Studies in the Life of the Church?" in Perrin and Hays, *Jesus, Paul and the People of God*, pp. 115-58 (p. 122).

in particular, in those ways easily generates readings that are unfaithful to the theological significance of texts that have other things to say than ideas that fit easily with Christology, the doctrine of the Trinity and the Rule of Faith.

Theological interpretation is an aspect of exegesis. It involves discerning the theological questions that are at issue in texts. When it seeks to set in a wider context the theological insights expressed in a text it will operate in a way that recognizes how Jesus is the decisive moment in God's fulfilling his purpose in the world, but it will expect to find that the texts also nuance our understanding of Jesus' significance. It will take into account the way the Christian tradition has understood the theological implications of Scripture, and it will reconsider its work if it finds itself coming to a conclusion that stands in tension with that tradition, but it will not assume that the same authority attaches to this doctrinal tradition as attaches to the Scriptures themselves. And it will make the assumption that the God who speaks and acts in the Scriptures is the God who is Father, Son and Holy Spirit, but it will not read that formulation into Scriptures, because that would skew what we might learn theologically from particular texts.

Kevin Vanhoozer suggests that "theological interpretation is biblical interpretation oriented to the knowledge of God."[56] I am not sure whether I agree with that statement. In principle I want people to reflect on the theological significance of texts even if they are not people who are interested in the knowledge of God. I learn from such people; I know that they can help to check what I think I see in texts and that they sometimes see things that I miss. When I am engaged in interpretation my work is an exercise in seeking to understand a text. I assume the reality of the God of whom it speaks and my study is indeed oriented to knowledge about God and knowledge of God, to acknowledgment of God and to service of God. In this sense my reading of Scripture has its ultimate focus not on the biblical text but on the divine Teacher, whom we are seeking to come to know and follow.[57] I am committed to accepting whatever I find in biblical texts, and there are disadvantages as well as advantages from occupying this position. I often think that students

[56]Kevin J. Vanhoozer, "What Is Theological Interpretation of the Bible?" in *Dictionary for Theological Interpretation of the Bible*, ed. Kevin J. Vanhoozer et al. (Grand Rapids: Baker, 2005), pp. 19-25 (p. 24).
[57]Levering, *Participatory Biblical Exegesis*, e.g., p. 63.

take the view that one of my jobs as a professor is to reassure them that the Bible does not say anything that they do not already think, and to show how when it says something outrageous it does not mean it. If theological interpretation is an aspect of academic study for which faith is not a requirement, then people who read texts without being personally interested in knowing God may enable me to see things I do not want to see.

The aim of interpretation is to enable the Scriptures to confront us, widen our thinking, reframe our thinking, rescue us from our narrowness and deliver us from the way our thinking and lives are decisively shaped by our being modern or postmodern, Western or non-Western people. The vocation of theological interpretation is to encourage that process and not let it be constrained by christocentrism, trinitarianism or an unqualified submission to the Christian tradition.

CONCLUSION

So do we need the New Testament? Or rather, what's new about the New Testament? Christians commonly operate with the working hypothesis that Jesus brought a revelation from God that went significantly beyond the revelation in the First Testament. My thesis in this volume has been that the chief significance of Jesus does not lie in any new revelation that he brought. It lies in who he was, what he did and what happened to him, and what he will do. He did not reveal new truths about what it means to be God except the fact that God is more complicated than people would previously have thought ("three persons and one God"). He did not reveal new truths about what it means to be human but (like a prophet) brought into sharper focus some of the truths that people ought to have known.

Thus their reaction to him was not, "Wow, we never knew that." It was more something along the lines of, "I wish you hadn't reminded us of that," and of, "What right have you got to be associating yourself with God so closely?" He did bring a concrete embodiment of who God had already told Israel that he was and had shown Israel that he was. In this sense Paul indeed implicitly thinks in terms of "a revelation which began with creation but which now has been brought into sharper focus in Christ."[1] Jesus provoked Jews and Gentiles to an ultimate rejection of God that God turned into the ultimate means whereby his relationship with his people could be affirmed, healed and restored. He also thus opened the way for the news about what he had done to be shared with the Gentile world as something that could

---

[1]James D. G. Dunn, *The Theology of Paul the Apostle* (Grand Rapids: Eerdmans, 1998), pp. 658-59.

bring it the same blessing, in keeping with God's original intention. And he established his own authority to be the person who would ultimately judge the world as a whole.

In the course of telling his story and working out its implications, the New Testament does make some affirmations that supplement what people could know from the First Testament. One is the fact that Sheol is not the end for humanity. At the end, all humanity is going to be raised from death in order to enjoy resurrection life or to go to hell. Thus people in the First Testament "did not receive what was promised. God had planned something better for us, so that they would not be brought to completion without us" (Heb 11:39-40). Paul pushes the argument further in connection with affirming that all God's people will be raised or will meet the Lord together (1 Thess 4:13-18). We do not go to heaven when we die; the entire people of God will reach completion together. Alongside this truth is the way the New Testament assumes the existence of Satan. While the First Testament presupposes the existence of an embodiment of resistance to God, the New Testament puts more emphasis on this motif.

It is appropriate that the truths about resurrection, hell and Satan should be associated with the story of Jesus' dying and rising. It was Jesus' dying and rising that made resurrection possible. It was these events that brought to a climax the conflict between God and the power that resists God. And it was these events that made hell necessary for people who turn their back on what God did in Jesus and insist on maintaining their resistant stance. Oddly, these truths were all part of Jewish thinking in Jesus' day, so that even they are not new revelations that Jesus brings. It is almost as if the people of God knew they needed to affirm these beliefs even though they couldn't quite know why or on what basis they might do so. It is Jesus who gives us reason to believe things that it would be nice to believe (at least some of them are nice to believe). He rescues us from just whistling in the dark and invites us to trust in him.

Name and Subject Index

Scripture Index

Finding the Textbook You Need

The IVP Academic Textbook Selector
is an online tool for instantly finding the IVP books
suitable for over 250 courses across 24 disciplines.

---

ivpacademic.com
